COOKING WITH

Bon Appétit

COOKING WITH
Bon Appétit

Picnics and Barbecues

THE KNAPP PRESS
Publishers
Los Angeles

Published by The Knapp Press
5900 Wilshire Boulevard, Los Angeles, California 90036

Library of Congress Cataloging in Publication Data

Main entry under title:

Picnics and barbecues.

  (Cooking with Bon appétit)
  Includes index.
  1. Outdoor cookery. 2. Barbecue cookery.
3. Menus. I. Bon appétit II. Series.
TX823.P53 1986   641.5'78   85-23986
ISBN 0-89535-174-9

On the cover (clockwise from left): *Barbecued Rabbit; Raised Meat Pie; Composed Summer Salad with Medallions of Smoked Rabbit*

Printed and bound in the United States of America

10   9   8   7   6   5   4   3

🍃 Contents

COOKING WITH
Bon Appétit

❦ *Introduction*

There are few more civilized ways to savor a lovely day—or evening—than with a leisurely alfresco meal. Just pack the picnic hamper or fire up the grill, and somehow even simple fare is transformed into something special. Picnics and barbecues are also among the easiest of entertainments, because nobody misses fancy appointments when the food is terrific, the setting is attractive and appetites are whetted by fresh air.

To keep the cook's job as simple as possible this book is organized in menu format, with dishes varying from sophisticated to bathing-suit casual. There are cozy lunches or suppers for two, family meals for four or six, convivial gatherings for eight, 10 or 12—in short, meals suitable for nearly any size or style of outdoor party. Of course, the multi-course menus can be pared down as you wish. For example, if time is short you may choose to buy the dessert ready-made or to skip an appetizer or home-baked bread. Several of the menus include suggestions for a simple accompaniment, such as fresh fruit or a tossed green salad, for which no recipe is given; in these cases the entry is made in italics.

Just about any picnic or barbecue is assured of success with a bit of advance planning. For safe transport, wrap breakables like wine glasses in napkins, then tuck them into the folds of the tablecloth. Be sure that each food container seals dependably, and if there is any doubt wrap it in a heavy-duty plastic bag. Prechill the containers for cold food and drinks; if you are bringing a hot soup or beverage, warm the vacuum bottle with boiling water. When packing the picnic basket, keep in mind how you will want to present each dish and include such garnishes as salad greens, parsley sprigs and lemon wedges. Remember, too, essentials like breadboard and knife, corkscrew, bottle opener, salt and pepper shakers, paper towels and a big trash bag for cleanup. If the meal is to be no farther than your backyard, even less preparation is needed—just turn to page 14 for hints that will make you a virtuoso at the grill.

No matter the site of a picnic or barbecue, there's always one cardinal rule: Bring along the right companions. With good food and good company, the rest is incidental.

Tex-Mex Cookout

Pico de Gallo
Texas-style Barbecued Chicken
Avocado-frosted Cauliflower Salad
Flour Tortillas
Corn Tortillas
Margarita Ice
Pecan Treats

Serves 8

Pico de Gallo (Rooster's Beak)

This subtle accompaniment to spicy food can be served as a salad.

8 servings

4 ripe avocados, peeled and cubed
2 medium tomatoes, peeled and cut same size as avocado cubes
1 medium-size white onion, finely minced
2 garlic cloves, minced

2 tablespoons chopped cilantro
1 to 2 serrano chilies, finely chopped
3 tablespoons fresh lemon juice
2 tablespoons olive oil
Salt and freshly ground pepper

Combine all ingredients and mix well. Cover and refrigerate 1 to 2 hours.

Texas-style Barbecued Chicken

8 servings

2 3½-pound chickens, split
Juice of 1 large lemon
4 garlic cloves, minced
¼ cup coarse salt

2 tablespoons sweet Hungarian paprika
2 teaspoons cayenne pepper

Rub chicken with lemon juice and garlic. Combine salt, paprika and pepper and sprinkle over skin. Place skin side up on wire rack(s) set over baking sheet(s) and refrigerate uncovered at least 8 hours or, preferably, overnight.

Preheat oven to 300°F. Bake chicken 1 hour. Meanwhile, prepare charcoal. Transfer chicken to barbecue and grill, turning occasionally, until meat is done and skin is crisp, about 15 minutes per side. Cut in half and arrange on platter.

Avocado-frosted Cauliflower Salad

8 servings

1 head cauliflower

Marinade
6 tablespoons vegetable oil
3 tablespoons white wine vinegar
Salt and freshly ground pepper

Sauce
3 medium avocados, peeled, pitted
and chopped

1 small onion, minced
Pinch of freshly grated nutmeg
Salt

Toasted sliced almonds
Lettuce leaves
Cherry tomatoes

Steam cauliflower until crisp-tender. Remove from steamer and set aside.
For marinade: Combine oil, vinegar, salt and pepper and pour over cauliflower while still warm. Chill overnight, turning once or twice. Drain, reserving 3 tablespoons marinade.
For sauce: Mash avocados with fork in medium bowl. Add onion, reserved marinade, nutmeg and salt and mix well.
Frost cauliflower completely. Cover with toasted almonds. Serve on bed of lettuce and garnish with cherry tomatoes.

Flour Tortillas

While experienced cooks can turn these out with no problem using a large skillet over medium-high heat, the first-time tortilla maker would do well to use an electric frypan or griddle.

Makes about 20

4 cups all purpose flour
½ cup solid vegetable shortening

2 teaspoons salt
1¼ cups warm water (115°F)

Sift flour into large bowl. Add shortening and rub with fingertips until consistency of coarse meal. Dissolve salt in warm water and add to flour in steady stream, using fingertips to blend. Knead in bowl until dough forms ball. Turn out onto lightly floured surface and knead about 3 minutes (*dough will not be smooth*). Cover with towel and let rest at room temperature 1 hour (or chill overnight).
Knead dough on work surface about 1 minute. Cover and let rest at room temperature 10 minutes.
Pinch off dough in 1½-inch pieces. Roll on lightly floured surface into 7-inch circle (roll outward from center but do not get edges too thin). Stack between pieces of waxed paper.
Heat electric skillet or griddle to 375°F, or place 10-inch skillet over medium-high heat. Cook tortilla, turning occasionally and pushing edges down with folded potholder or small towel so edges brown evenly and light brown spots appear on surface, about 2 to 3 minutes (*if using skillet over direct heat, cooking time will be less*). Transfer tortilla to plate and cover with cloth napkin or towel to keep warm. Repeat with remaining dough, wiping out any flour in skillet as necessary. Just before serving, wrap tortillas in foil and reheat in 250°F oven or steamer about 5 minutes.

Corn Tortillas

Makes about 16

2 cups masa harina

1½ cups warm water (115°F)

Measure masa harina into large mixing bowl. Using hands, gradually work in water until mixture forms solid mass (you will need to adjust water to achieve a workable dough; it should be firm but not dry or crumbly).

To test: Pinch off enough dough to roll between palms into 1½-inch ball. Cut open 2 long sides of plastic sandwich bag. Lay one half on bottom of tortilla press. Place ball of dough in center of press and fold other half of bag over top. Close press to flatten dough.

Remove tortilla and plastic. Hold tortilla in your hand and peel off one side of plastic; turn and peel off other half of bag. (*If dough is too dry, cracks will form around edges of tortilla; if it is too moist, plastic will not peel off without tearing the tortilla. Adjust consistency of remaining dough as necessary, adding more masa harina or warm water, and test again.*)

Roll remaining dough into 1½-inch balls. Press 5 or 6 into tortilla shape and line up on work surface.

Lightly oil electric skillet or griddle and preheat to 375°F (or lightly oil 10-inch skillet and place over medium-high heat). Cook tortilla 1 minute; turn and cook 30 seconds on other side. Transfer to towel-lined basket, cover lightly and keep warm. If necessary, wrap tortillas in foil and reheat in oven or steamer 5 minutes before serving.

Margarita Ice

10 to 12 servings

2 cups fresh lime juice
(reserve shells)
3 cups sugar
2 cups water
Finely grated peel of 3 limes

3 egg whites

Sugar
1 cup white tequila
½ cup orange liqueur
Lime slices and mint sprigs

Pour lime juice into ice cream maker. Combine sugar, water and lime peel in heavy 3-quart saucepan. Bring to boil and cook without stirring until syrup reaches 234°F (thread stage) on candy thermometer, about 5 to 7 minutes. Set pan in large bowl of ice water and stir syrup with wooden spoon until cooled to lukewarm. Blend into lime juice.

Fill ice cream freezer with mixture of 8 parts ice to 1 part rock salt. Freeze lime mixture according to manufacturer's instructions until just partially frozen (this should take about 20 minutes).

Meanwhile, beat egg whites in mixing bowl until stiff peaks form. Spoon over lime mixture and continue churning until firm, about 10 minutes. Remove container and transfer to freezer.

To serve, scoop ice into glasses and top with small amount of tequila and liqueur. Garnish with lime slices and mint.

Pecan Treats

Makes 2 dozen

Crust
½ cup (1 stick) butter, room temperature
3 ounces cream cheese, room temperature
1 cup sifted all purpose flour

Filling
¾ cup firmly packed light brown sugar

1 egg, beaten to blend
1 tablespoon butter, room temperature
1 teaspoon vanilla
Pinch of salt

⅔ cup coarsely chopped pecans (about 2½ ounces)

For crust: Cream butter with cream cheese in medium bowl. Blend in flour. Refrigerate dough while preparing filling.

For filling: Combine brown sugar, egg, butter, vanilla and salt in medium bowl of electric mixer and beat well.

Preheat oven to 325°F. Shape dough into 24 balls 1 inch in diameter. Press onto bottoms and sides of 1¾-inch muffin tins. Sprinkle with ⅓ cup pecans.

Spoon filling into tins. Sprinkle with remaining ⅓ cup pecans. Bake until filling is set and crust is golden, about 25 minutes. Cool in pan on wire rack. Store in airtight container.

Picnic à la Russe

Quick Borscht
Piroshki
Russian Black Bread
Lettuceless Salad
Russian Cream

Serves 6

Quick Borscht

6 servings

1 16-ounce jar red cabbage, undrained
1 16-ounce can julienne of beets, undrained
1 10¾-ounce can beef broth

2 tablespoons white wine vinegar
Pinch of cayenne pepper
Sour cream and fresh dill or dried dillweed (optional)

Combine first 5 ingredients in large bowl. Cover and chill until ready to serve. Garnish with sour cream and dill, if desired.
Soup can also be served warm.

Piroshki

Makes about 20

Pastry
- 2 cups all purpose flour
- 1/2 cup (1 stick) chilled unsalted butter, cut into 1/4-inch pieces
- 1/4 cup chilled solid vegetable shortening
- 1/4 teaspoon salt
- 4 to 6 tablespoons ice water

Filling
- 2 tablespoons (1/4 stick) butter
- 1 1/2 cups finely chopped onion
- 12 ounces ground beef
- 2 hard-cooked eggs, minced
- 3 tablespoons snipped fresh dill or 1 1/2 teaspoons dried dillweed
  Salt and freshly ground pepper

- 1 egg beaten with 1 tablespoon water

For pastry: Combine flour, butter, shortening and salt in large bowl. Mix with pastry blender until consistency of coarse meal. Sprinkle with 4 tablespoons water and mix quickly until dough can be gathered into ball; if dough does not hold together, add remaining ice water a little at a time until ball is formed. Wrap and refrigerate 1 hour.

For filling: Melt 2 tablespoons butter in heavy skillet over medium heat. Add onion and cook, stirring occasionally, until soft but not brown, about 8 to 10 minutes. Crumble meat into skillet. Increase heat to high and cook until meat is no longer pink. Let cool. Chop finely in processor or by hand, or force through meat grinder. Transfer to bowl and mix in eggs, dill, salt and pepper.

Turn dough out onto lightly floured surface and roll into rectangle. Fold into thirds (as for letter). Turn and roll again into rectangle. Repeat rolling and folding 3 more times. Wrap with plastic and refrigerate for 1 hour.

Roll out dough to thickness of 1/8 inch. Using 3 1/2-inch round cutter, cut out as many circles as possible. Gather pastry scraps into ball and roll again, cutting into additional circles.

Preheat oven to 400°F. Grease baking sheet. Place about 1 tablespoon filling on each round, pressing with back of spoon to flatten filling slightly. Fold upper side of dough down over filling. Fold in the two sides, then fold bottom up and over, pressing to close. Place seam side down on baking sheet and brush with beaten egg. Bake until pastry is golden brown, about 30 to 40 minutes. Serve piroshki warm or cool.

Russian Black Bread

Serve with sweet butter; also great with sour cream and caviar, or with cream cheese and smoked salmon.

Makes 2 round loaves

- 2 cups water
- 1/4 cup molasses
- 1/4 cup cider vinegar
- 1/4 cup (1/2 stick) unsalted butter
- 1 ounce unsweetened chocolate

- 2 envelopes dry yeast
- 1 tablespoon sugar
- 1/2 cup warm water (105°F to 115°F)

- 3 cups unbleached all purpose flour or bread flour
- 3 cups medium rye flour*

- 1/2 cup whole wheat flour
- 1 cup unprocessed bran flakes
- 2 tablespoons caraway seeds
- 1 tablespoon salt
- 2 teaspoons instant coffee powder
- 2 teaspoons minced shallot
- 1/2 teaspoon fennel seeds
  Additional unbleached all purpose flour

  Cornmeal or semolina

Heat 2 cups water, molasses, vinegar, butter and chocolate in heavy small saucepan over low heat until butter and chocolate melt, stirring frequently. Cool to 105°F to 115°F.

Sprinkle yeast and sugar over warm water in small bowl; stir to dissolve. Let stand until foamy, about 10 minutes.

Mix all purpose, rye and whole wheat flours in medium bowl. Measure 2 cups flour mixture into large bowl of heavy electric mixer fitted with paddle. Add bran, caraway, salt, coffee, shallot and fennel. Blend in vinegar and yeast mixtures on low speed until smooth. Increase speed to medium and mix 5 minutes to develop gluten. Decrease speed to low and stir in enough remaining flour mixture ½ cup at a time to form dough that pulls away from sides of bowl. Knead dough on floured surface until just smooth and elastic, about 3 minutes, kneading in additional all purpose flour if very sticky; dough will be tacky.

Grease large bowl. Add dough, turning to coat entire surface. Cover bowl with plastic. Let rise in warm draft-free area until doubled, about 1 hour.

Sprinkle 2 baking sheets with cornmeal. Gently knead dough on lightly floured surface until deflated. Cut in half. Knead each piece into round. Place on prepared sheets. Cover with waxed paper or towel. Let rise in warm area until doubled in volume, about 45 minutes.

Preheat oven to 350°F. Slash X in top of loaves using serrated knife. Bake until well browned and loaves sound hollow when tapped on bottom, about 50 minutes. Immediately transfer to racks. Cool completely before slicing.

*Available at natural foods stores.

Lettuceless Salad

6 main-course or 12 side-dish servings

Herbed Dressing (makes about 3½ cups)
- 1 egg
- 1 tablespoon white vinegar
- 2 teaspoons Dijon mustard
- 1 small garlic clove, halved
- 1 teaspoon dill seeds
- ¾ teaspoon salt
- ½ teaspoon each dried thyme, marjoram and basil, crumbled
- ½ teaspoon celery salt
- ¼ teaspoon freshly ground white pepper
- ½ cup vegetable oil
- 1 cup buttermilk
- 2 cups mayonnaise, preferably homemade

Salad
- 1 head broccoli, cut into florets
- 1 head cauliflower, cut into florets
- 1 pound cheddar cheese, cut into small cubes
- 4 celery stalks, sliced
- 3 large carrots, sliced
- 1 cucumber, cut into large cubes
- 1 red apple (unpeeled), cored and cut into large cubes
- 1 small onion, cut into small cubes
- 1 green bell pepper, seeded and sliced
- ⅓ cup raisins
- 1 cup salted roasted sunflower seeds

For dressing: Combine egg, vinegar, mustard, garlic and seasoning in processor and blend well. With machine running, pour oil and then buttermilk through feed tube and process until smooth and thick. Transfer mixture to large bowl. Whisk in mayonnaise.

For salad: Combine all ingredients except sunflower seeds in large salad bowl and toss well. Divide among individual plates and spoon some of dressing over. Garnish with sunflower seeds. Pass remaining dressing.

Russian Cream

For a picnic, try serving this in unbreakable plastic Champagne glasses.

6 to 8 servings

¾ cup superfine sugar
½ cup water
1 envelope unflavored gelatin
1 cup whipping cream

1½ cups crème fraîche or sour cream
1 teaspoon vanilla
  Sliced strawberries and
  blueberries

Combine sugar, water and gelatin in small saucepan and blend well. Let stand 4 to 5 minutes. Place over medium heat and bring to boil, stirring constantly. Remove from heat. Gradually blend in cream. Combine crème fraîche and vanilla in medium bowl. Gradually add hot sugar mixture, whisking constantly until smooth. Pour into 6 to 8 wine glasses or dessert dishes. Cover and refrigerate 4 to 6 hours. Garnish with sliced strawberries and blueberries.

Mediterranean Picnic

Cold Mint-Cucumber Soup
Turkish Lamb and Pine Nut Borek
Greek-style Salad
Marinated Carrot Salad
Olives Marinated with Orange and Fennel
Fresh fruit, dried fruit and nuts

Serves 4 to 6

Cold Mint-Cucumber Soup

A delicate and unusual combination that is refreshing on a hot day.

4 to 6 servings

3 tablespoons butter
1 medium onion, finely chopped
1 small garlic clove, minced
3 medium cucumbers, peeled
  and thinly sliced
3 tablespoons flour (preferably
  rice flour)
2 cups chicken stock

2 tablespoons finely chopped
  fresh mint
1 cup half and half
1 cup plain yogurt
  Salt and freshly ground
  white pepper
  Sliced cucumber (garnish)

Melt butter in large skillet over medium heat. Add onion and garlic and sauté until limp but not brown. Add sliced cucumber and cook slowly until soft. Remove from heat. Stir in flour, then stock, blending well. Place over medium-high heat and bring to boil. Reduce heat and simmer 5 minutes. Transfer to processor or blender in batches and puree. Pour into bowl and blend in mint. Cover and chill well. Just before serving, stir in half and half and yogurt and mix well. Taste and season with salt and pepper. Garnish each serving with sliced cucumber.

Turkish Lamb and Pine Nut Borek

Makes 6 rolls

2 tablespoons olive oil
1 onion, finely chopped
12 ounces ground lamb
1 garlic clove, minced
1 tablespoon tomato paste
  Pinch of dried marjoram,
  crumbled
  Pinch of cinnamon
  Salt and freshly ground pepper

1 egg, beaten
¼ cup pine nuts, sautéed in butter
  until golden

6 sheets phyllo dough
  (12 × 18 inches)
6 tablespoons (¾ stick) unsalted
  butter, melted

Heat oil in large skillet over medium-high heat. Add onion and sauté until translucent. Stir in lamb and garlic and sauté until meat is well browned and crumbly, draining off fat as it accumulates. Stir in tomato paste and season with marjoram, cinnamon, salt and pepper. Reduce heat and simmer gently 5 minutes. Let stand until cool, then blend in egg and pine nuts.

Preheat oven to 400°F. Lightly grease baking sheet. Place 1 sheet of phyllo on work surface and brush half with some of melted butter. Fold lengthwise into 9 × 12-inch rectangle. Brush again with butter. Spoon about ⅓ cup filling to within 1½ inches of bottom and sides of phyllo. Fold in long edges about 1¼ inches, then brush folds with butter. Roll to enclose filling (the roll will be about 6 inches long). Transfer to baking sheet. Repeat with remaining phyllo and filling. Brush all rolls with butter. Bake until golden brown, about 15 minutes. Let cool on wire rack. Serve warm or at "picnic" temperature.

Borek can be made ahead and frozen. When ready to use, thaw and reheat in preheated 375°F oven until crisp, about 10 minutes.

Greek-style Salad

4 to 6 servings

2 medium tomatoes, cored and
  cut into wedges
1 medium zucchini, cut into
  matchstick julienne
1 cucumber, sliced
1 cup pitted black olives
1 medium-size red onion, thinly
  sliced and separated into rings

8 ounces feta cheese, cubed
1 6-ounce jar artichoke hearts
  with marinade
¼ cup red wine vinegar
  Freshly ground pepper

Combine tomatoes, zucchini and cucumber in large bowl. Add olives, onion rings and feta cheese. Top with artichoke hearts and marinade. Pour red wine vinegar over salad, sprinkle with pepper and toss well. Chill several hours or overnight; toss occasionally. Serve at room temperature.

Marinated Carrot Salad

Makes 2¾ cups

½ cup red wine vinegar
½ cup sugar
3 tablespoons vegetable oil
1 teaspoon Worcestershire sauce

1 teaspoon Dijon mustard
1 pound carrots, peeled
  and shredded

Combine vinegar, sugar, oil, Worcestershire and mustard in medium bowl and mix well. Add carrots and toss to coat. Cover and refrigerate overnight, tossing once or twice. Drain carrots well before serving.

Olives Marinated with Orange and Fennel

Start these zesty olives the day before serving. If using olives packed in brine, rinse them well before combining with the remaining ingredients.

Makes 2 pounds

2 pounds black olives

1 cup fresh lemon juice
  Peel from 2 lemons (yellow part only), cut into long thin strips

Peel from 2 oranges (orange part only), cut into long thin strips
¼ cup fennel seeds
4 large garlic cloves

Combine all ingredients in wide-mouthed jar. Cover tightly and turn jar over several times. Marinate overnight at room temperature before serving, turning jar occasionally.

Cool Alfresco Lunch

Marinated Artichokes
Cold Stuffed Veal Roll
New Potato Salad
Basket of cherry tomatoes
Herb and Onion Bread Braids
Walnut Butter Crisps
Fresh fruit

Serves 2

Marinated Artichokes

Orange juice and herbs combine for a distinctively different marinade.

2 servings

2 artichokes, cooked

Marinade
¹/₂ cup fresh orange juice
¹/₄ cup olive oil
2 tablespoons tarragon vinegar
2 tablespoons chopped shallot or green onion
1 tablespoon minced fresh parsley
1¹/₂ teaspoons grated orange peel
¹/₂ teaspoon salt
Pinch *each* of sugar and dried tarragon, basil and chervil
¹/₄ teaspoon dry mustard
¹/₄ teaspoon Worcestershire sauce

Cut artichokes in half from tip to stem. Remove choke and small inner leaves.

Combine all ingredients for marinade in medium bowl and blend well. Add artichokes, turning several times to coat. Cover and refrigerate overnight.

Transfer artichokes and marinade* to jar or other tightly covered container if transporting. Serve artichokes with some of marinade spooned over top.

*Reserve 2 tablespoons marinade for Tangy Lemon Sauce for veal roll.

Cold Stuffed Veal Roll

The roll can be prepared a day ahead; make the sauce on the morning of the picnic.

2 servings

4 ounces untrimmed pork
2 ounces veal
¹/₄ cup freshly grated Parmesan or dry Monterey Jack cheese
¹/₄ cup chopped cooked spinach (squeezed dry)
1 small egg, beaten
1 teaspoon salt
¹/₈ teaspoon dried thyme, crumbled
¹/₈ teaspoon dried marjoram, crumbled

2 slices firm-textured white bread (crusts trimmed), torn into pieces
¹/₃ cup milk

1 tablespoon butter
¹/₄ cup finely chopped onion
¹/₄ cup pistachio nuts

1 1-pound veal round steak
¹/₂ chicken breast, skinned, boned and cut into ¹/₂-inch strips
1 hard-cooked egg, halved lengthwise

1 quart (4 cups) rich chicken stock
1 quart (4 cups) water
1 cup dry white wine or vermouth
1 onion, quartered
2 garlic cloves
1 bay leaf
Parsley sprigs and lemon slices
Tangy Lemon Sauce*

Grind pork with veal twice using meat grinder fitted with blade. Transfer to bowl of electric mixer. Add cheese, spinach, egg, salt, thyme and marjoram and blend.

Combine bread and milk and let stand several minutes, stirring occasionally.

Meanwhile, melt butter in small skillet over low heat. Add onion and cook until transparent, about 5 to 7 minutes; do not brown. Squeeze bread dry and add to meat mixture with onion. Mix at high speed until light and fluffy. Gently fold in nuts, blending thoroughly.

Cut cheesecloth into 10 × 13-inch piece. Pound veal between 2 sheets of waxed paper into rectangle about 8 × 11 inches. Position on cheesecloth so there is 2-inch border on all sides. Spread half of meat mixture in strip down one long side of veal. Arrange chicken strips over filling and top with egg. Cover with remaining filling. Roll up veal lengthwise, using cheesecloth as aid. Secure ends of cheesecloth with string and tie around veal 3 or 4 times.

Combine stock, water, wine, onion, garlic and bay leaf in 5- to 6-quart saucepan or Dutch oven large enough to accommodate veal. Set veal in pan; if liquid does not cover, add water. Place over high heat and bring to boil. Reduce heat, cover and simmer until tender, about 1 1/4 hours. Remove veal from pan and cool to room temperature. Discard string and cheesecloth. Wrap veal in plastic or foil and chill thoroughly. Transfer to platter and slice with very thin knife. Garnish with parsley and lemon. Serve with sauce.

*Tangy Lemon Sauce

Makes about ³/₄ cup

1/2 cup mayonnaise
2 tablespoons artichoke marinade (see previous recipe)

Juice of 1/2 lemon
Finely grated peel of 1 lemon

Combine all ingredients in small bowl and blend well. Chill before serving.

New Potato Salad

The potatoes can be cooked one to two days ahead, drained, covered and chilled. Use small red new potatoes or any other firm, waxy type; the baking variety is not good for this salad.

2 servings

1 pound new potatoes

1/2 cup sour cream
1 teaspoon prepared horseradish
1/2 teaspoon Dijon mustard
Juice of 1/2 lemon
Salt and freshly ground pepper

1 ounce prosciutto, chopped
1 ounce Swiss or Gruyère cheese, cut into julienne (about 1/4 cup)
2 tablespoons minced fresh parsley

Bring large pot of salted water to rapid boil over high heat. Add potatoes, reduce heat to medium and simmer until tender but still firm (cooking time will depend on size and type of potatoes used). Drain well and pat dry. Let cool. (*Can be prepared 1 to 2 days ahead to this point. Cover potatoes and chill until ready to slice.*) If using red potatoes, do not peel; other potatoes should be peeled. Cut potatoes into thin slices.

Combine sour cream, horseradish, mustard, lemon juice, salt and pepper in large bowl and blend well. Add potato slices and toss to coat with dressing. Gently stir in prosciutto, cheese and parsley. Cover and chill. Let stand at room temperature for approximately 30 minutes before serving.

Herb and Onion Bread Braids

Makes 2 small loaves

1 tablespoon butter
1/2 medium onion, chopped (about 1/2 cup)
1 garlic clove, minced
2 tablespoons minced fresh parsley
1/2 teaspoon dried marjoram
1/4 teaspoon dried sage
1/4 teaspoon dried thyme

1/2 cup warm water (105°F to 115°F)
1 1/2 teaspoons dry yeast

1/2 teaspoon salt
1/2 teaspoon sugar
2 to 2 1/2 cups bread flour
2 tablespoons (1/4 stick) butter, room temperature

1 egg, beaten
Coarse salt (optional)

Oil large bowl and set aside. Melt 1 tablespoon butter in medium skillet over low heat. Add onion, garlic and herbs and cook until onion is translucent, about 5 minutes. Let cool.

Combine water, yeast, salt and sugar in another large bowl. Let stand until foamy, about 5 minutes. Add 1 cup flour, onion mixture and 2 tablespoons butter and beat well. Add enough remaining flour to form soft dough. Turn out onto lightly floured surface and knead about 5 minutes. Transfer to prepared bowl, turning to coat all surfaces. Cover bowl and let dough stand in warm draft-free area until doubled in volume, about 1½ hours.

Lightly grease baking sheet and set aside. Punch dough down, turn out onto work surface and knead lightly. Divide dough into 6 equal portions. Shape each into strand about ¾ inch in diameter and 8 to 9 inches long. Pinch 3 strands together at one end, sprinkling with water if necessary to make strands adhere. Braid dough strands, pinching other ends together firmly. Repeat with remaining 3 strands to make 2 loaves.

Transfer loaves to prepared baking sheet. Cover with towel. Let stand in warm draft-free area until doubled in volume, about 45 minutes to 1 hour.

Preheat oven to 425°F. Brush loaves with egg and sprinkle with coarse salt if desired. Bake until loaves are golden brown and sound hollow when tapped, 20 to 30 minutes. Cool on racks.

Walnut Butter Crisps

These can be baked ahead and kept airtight.

Makes about 2 dozen

6 tablespoons (¾ stick) unsalted butter, room temperature
¼ cup sugar
½ cup finely ground walnuts

½ teaspoon vanilla
1 cup all purpose flour
Pinch of salt

Preheat oven to 350°F. Lightly grease baking sheet and set aside. Cream butter with sugar in medium bowl. Stir in nuts and vanilla. Add flour and salt and blend well. Shape mixture into ¾-inch balls. Arrange on prepared baking sheet. Using bottom of glass covered with damp cloth, flatten balls to form circles about 1½ inches in diameter. Bake until lightly browned around edges, about 15 minutes. Transfer to rack and cool completely.

Southwest Grill Supper

Chilled White Bean and Buttermilk Soup
Grilled Pork Fajitas with Chiles Chipotles
Marinated Vegetable Salad in a Jar
Mexican Chocolate Ice Cream

Serves 6

Chilled White Bean and Buttermilk Soup

6 servings

8 ounces dried Great Northern
  beans, sorted

3 tablespoons butter
2 large carrots, quartered
1 medium onion, finely chopped
2 bay leaves
1½ teaspoons dried thyme, crumbled

6 cups chicken stock
1 teaspoon salt

1 cup (or more) buttermilk
¼ cup strained fresh lemon juice

Thin lemon slices
Minced fresh chives

Cover beans with cold water by 2 inches and soak 24 hours.

Melt butter in heavy large saucepan over medium-low heat. Add carrots, onion, bay leaves and thyme. Cover and cook until vegetables are golden, stirring occasionally, about 20 minutes.

Drain beans. Add to vegetables. Stir in stock and bring to boil, skimming foam from surface. Reduce heat, cover partially and simmer until beans are just tender, stirring occasionally, about 45 minutes. Add salt and simmer until beans

 ## *Hints for the Charcoal Chef: Perfect Fire, Perfect Timing, Perfect Food*

There is something singularly satisfying about the aroma and flavor of meats, seafood and vegetables that have been lovingly basted and cooked to golden-brown perfection over glowing coals. Mastering the age-old technique of barbecuing is not complicated but it does require meticulous attention to detail. First, there is the fire—it must be hot enough and it must have staying power. Then there are the seasonings, sauces and marinades to add just the right flavor accent and increase tenderness. And the proper equipment is also invaluable. Finally, there is the all-important matter of timing. Foods should be cooked until they are crusty on the outside and moist and flavorful within. Using the guidelines offered here for each of these steps, every cook will find that outdoor cooking is more fun and more exciting than ever.

The technique for building a perfect fire can inspire heated argument among old friends and good neighbors. Some advocate the primitive Outward Bound approach while others endorse such tools as electric starters and concealed gas jets. But the real secret of a successful fire is building one that is the right size for the job at hand. How you get it started is less important than the number of briquettes you use and letting them reach the stage where they are covered with a gray ash and glowing red inside. This usually takes 30 to 45 minutes to achieve. The number of briquettes varies not only with the kinds of foods you are cooking but with the amounts. If you are doing small amounts of quick-cooking meats (hamburger and shish kebab), seafood or vegetables, you will need about 12 to 15 briquettes. For longer-cooking foods (chicken, pork, roasts) or large amounts, use 24 to 32 briquettes. Set them alight (we leave the technique up to you) and let them burn until the gray-ash stage.

A safe rule to follow when barbecuing is do not rush. The slower your timing when you cook meat, fish or poultry, the juicier, tenderer and tastier the results will be.

Very little in the way of special equipment is needed to become a master of the barbecue. Here are the essentials:

are very tender, 15 minutes to 1 hour, depending on dryness of beans. Remove from heat.

Drain beans, reserving liquid. Discard carrots and bay leaves. Puree beans and 1 cup liquid in blender until smooth. Add remaining liquid and blend until smooth. Transfer to bowl. Stir in 1 cup buttermilk and lemon juice. Cover and refrigerate until very cold, at least 4 hours or overnight.

Just before serving, thin soup with more buttermilk if desired. Ladle into bowls. Garnish with lemon and chives.

Tongs—Since meat, poultry and fish should never be pierced as they cook (all those lovely juices are released into the fire rather than onto your plate), tongs are essential for turning and lifting. Choose a pair 16 to 18 inches long that has an insulated grip.

Pastry brush—Use one made of natural bristles or feathers. These are perfect for brushing a hot grill with oil (to keep foods from sticking) or for basting with sauces and marinades. Stay away from plastic bristle brushes, which shrivel and give off an unpleasant taste.

Hand-held grill—Helpful for turning fragile foods such as fish.

Seasoning comes from bastes, marinades, sauces and from adding branches of herbs, pine or fruit trees to the fire. One important fact to remember is that barbecued foods ask for lusty seasonings: Delicate flavorings can get lost in this form of cooking. Adding seasoning to the fire is called smoking, and it is a technique that has been with us for centuries as a way to add flavor and to preserve. We've discovered that smoking goes beyond hickory and hardwood chips, opening up a world of possibilities. Any fresh herb, fruit leaf (peach, apple, pear, apricot or citrus) or sprigs of pine can add exciting dimensions to meats, fish, poultry or vegetables. Be sure to soak leaves and branches in water before adding so that you will get smoke rather than more fire. Fresh or dried juniper berries, whole sweet spices such as cinnamon stick, aniseed, allspice, cloves or nutmeg (use sparingly) can add a wonderful touch to poultry, pork, lamb or game. The variations are myriad.

If fresh herbs aren't available, resolve to raise your own or—for a reasonable substitute—soak a quantity of dry herb (four or five tablespoons) in a small amount of water for about 15 minutes.

As a general guide, add smoking materials during the last 15 to 20 minutes of cooking. In the case of thick roasts or large, whole poultry, smoke for 45 minutes to an hour. The longer you smoke, the more intense the flavor.

Now that we have our fire down to a rosy glow, let's do some barbecuing!

Grilled Pork Fajitas with Chiles Chipotles

6 to 8 servings

1 35-ounce can Italian plum tomatoes, undrained
4 chiles chipotles (packed in adobo sauce),* including 1 tablespoon sauce
1 teaspoon salt
5 green onions, thickly sliced
1 cup finely chopped cilantro

1 2½- to 3-pound boneless pork loin, trimmed

¼ cup olive oil
4½ tablespoons fresh lime juice
2 teaspoons ground cumin
2 large garlic cloves, mashed

2 large ripe avocados
6 to 8 flour tortillas

Combine tomatoes and juice, chiles and sauce and salt in heavy medium saucepan and bring to boil over medium heat. Reduce heat and simmer until thick, stirring occasionally and breaking up tomatoes and chiles using wooden spoon, about 40 minutes. Add green onions and simmer 5 minutes. Remove from heat. Stir in cilantro. Cool sauce to room temperature. (*Can be prepared 2 days ahead and refrigerated. Bring to room temperature before using.*)

Discard thin strip of fatty meat from one side of pork. Slice pork into 18 to 24 ¼-inch pieces. Blend oil, 3 tablespoons lime juice, cumin and garlic in small bowl. Dip each slice of pork into mixture, then transfer pork to medium bowl. Pour any remaining mixture over pork. Let stand at room temperature 1 hour, stirring twice.

Prepare barbecue grill with very hot coals. Position rack 6 inches from coals. Arrange pork on rack and grill until lightly browned and no pink remains, about 3 minutes per side.

Peel, pit and coarsely mash avocados. Stir in remaining 1½ tablespoons lime juice. Heat tortillas on grill or in low oven. To assemble each fajita, spoon about ¼ cup avocado down center of each tortilla. Arrange 3 pork slices atop avocado. Cover with 1 to 2 tablespoons sauce. Fold up bottom of tortilla slightly and then fold in sides. Serve fajitas immediately.

*Available at Latin American markets. Fresh or canned green jalapeños can be substituted. Do not use dried chiles chipotles.

Marinated Vegetable Salad in a Jar

10 appetizer or 6 salad servings

½ cup red wine vinegar
1 tablespoon mustard seeds
1 teaspoon salt
2 cups olive oil
¾ cup minced Italian parsley

3 quarts water
6 new potatoes
1 tablespoon salt

3 garlic cloves
3 large bay leaves
2 small fresh or dried hot red chilies
1 cup Niçoise olives, drained

4 large celery stalks, cut diagonally into ½-inch pieces

6 green onions, trimmed to 5 inches
12 small mushrooms

4 medium carrots, cut diagonally into ½-inch pieces

2 cups cauliflower florets

Blend vinegar, mustard seed and salt in bowl. Whisk in oil in thin stream. Stir parsley into vinaigrette.

Combine water and potatoes in medium saucepan and bring to boil. Stir in 1 tablespoon salt. Reduce heat and simmer until potatoes are just tender, about 10 minutes. Using slotted spoon, transfer potatoes to wide-mouthed half-gallon jar with tight-fitting lid. Reserve water and keep hot.

Pour ⅓ of vinaigrette over potatoes. Place 1 garlic clove, 1 bay leaf and 1 red chili between potatoes and side of jar. Sprinkle olives over potatoes.

Bring reserved water to boil. Add celery and cook until crisp-tender, about 3 minutes. Using slotted spoon, transfer celery to jar, spreading evenly over olives. Keep water hot.

Push green onions down between vegetables and side of jar, spacing evenly. Arrange mushrooms over celery. Pour ⅓ of vinaigrette over vegetables.

Bring reserved water to boil. Add carrots and cook until crisp-tender, about 5 minutes. Using slotted spoon, transfer carrots to jar, spreading evenly over mushrooms. Keep water hot. Place 1 garlic clove, 1 bay leaf and remaining red chili between vegetables and jar.

Bring reserved water to boil. Add cauliflower and cook until crisp-tender, about 4 minutes. Using slotted spoon, transfer cauliflower to jar. Add remaining vinaigrette, garlic clove and bay leaf. (Contents should reach top of jar. If not, add more vegetables.) Cool salad to room temperature.

Close jar tightly. Refrigerate at least 48 hours or up to 1 week, turning jar twice daily to coat vegetables with vinaigrette. To serve, pour salad into large bowl and toss gently.

Mexican Chocolate Ice Cream

Makes 1½ to 2 quarts

8 ounces milk chocolate (preferably imported), chopped

3 cups half and half
1 cup whipping cream
4 egg yolks

¾ cup sugar
1 teaspoon cinnamon
1½ tablespoons vanilla

1 cup toasted almonds*

Melt chocolate in double boiler over gently simmering water. Stir until smooth. Remove from over water.

Bring half and half and cream to boil in heavy large saucepan. Whisk yolks in large bowl until foamy. Combine sugar and cinnamon. Slowly add to yolks and whisk until mixture is thick and lemon colored. Whisk half and half mixture into yolks. Return to saucepan and cook over low heat until mixture thickens and leaves path on back of wooden spoon when finger is drawn across, stirring constantly, about 7 minutes. Transfer to bowl. Vigorously whisk in melted chocolate and vanilla; mixture will appear grainy. Cover and chill custard at least 3 hours, stirring occasionally.

Transfer to ice cream maker and process according to manufacturer's instructions. Stir in almonds. Freeze in covered container several hours to mellow. Let ice cream soften slightly in refrigerator before serving.

*If serving ice cream more than 24 hours after preparation, omit toasted almonds (they become soggy) and use ¼ teaspoon almond extract instead. Add extract to custard along with vanilla.

New England Patio Dinner

Brown's Daiquiris
New England Lobster Spread
Herbed Zucchini and Pea Soup
Summer Garden Salad
Grilled Swordfish with Mustard Sauce
Tomatoes Filled with Corn Pudding
Portuguese Sweet Bread
Strawberries on the Half Shell

Serves 8

Brown's Daiquiris

8 servings

Crushed ice
1 cup fresh lemon juice
10 tablespoons sugar

2 cups white rum
Fresh mint sprigs

Fill 8 large glasses with crushed ice. Combine lemon juice and sugar in pitcher and stir until sugar dissolves. Blend in rum. Pour into prepared glasses. Garnish with mint and serve.

New England Lobster Spread

A simple but luxurious appetizer.

8 servings

8 ounces cooked lobster meat, finely chopped
½ cup mayonnaise, preferably homemade

Chopped green onion or chives
Freshly ground pepper
Crackers

Combine all ingredients except crackers. Pack into decorative bowl. Cover and chill 2 hours. Serve with crackers.

Herbed Zucchini and Pea Soup

Especially good paired with the Portuguese Sweet Bread.

8 servings

2 cups chicken stock
4 small onions, thinly sliced
¼ cup minced fresh parsley
¼ teaspoon minced fresh chervil
¼ teaspoon minced fresh oregano
  Salt and freshly ground pepper
4 medium zucchini, thinly sliced

2 cups shelled fresh peas
  (about 2 pounds unshelled)

2 tablespoons sugar
2 teaspoons prepared horseradish
1 teaspoon fresh lemon juice
2 cups half and half

  Lemon and zucchini rounds

Combine chicken stock, onions, parsley, chervil, oregano and salt and pepper to taste in large saucepan and bring to boil. Add zucchini and boil until tender, about 5 minutes. Transfer mixture to blender.

Cook peas in boiling salted water until tender. Drain. Add to blender and puree until smooth. Add sugar, horseradish and lemon juice and blend thoroughly. Mix in half and half. Cover and refrigerate at least 5 hours.

Adjust seasoning with salt and pepper. Ladle soup into bowls. Garnish with lemon and zucchini rounds.

Summer Garden Salad

Crisp and colorful.

8 servings

¼ cup red wine vinegar
⅛ to ¼ teaspoon dry mustard
1 small garlic clove, minced
¾ cup olive oil
  Salt and freshly ground pepper
2 cups yellow wax beans or green beans, cut into 2-inch lengths and blanched
1 cup cauliflower florets

1 bunch watercress, stemmed and coarsely chopped
1 bunch green onions, chopped
1 medium cucumber, peeled and coarsely chopped
1 medium-size red bell pepper, seeded and coarsely chopped
16 radishes, thinly sliced

Blend vinegar, mustard and garlic in small bowl. Whisk in oil in thin stream. Season dressing with salt and pepper. Combine remaining ingredients in large bowl. Add dressing and toss well. Chill 1 hour before serving.

Grilled Swordfish with Mustard Sauce

8 servings

Swordfish
8 8-ounce swordfish steaks, about 1 inch thick
¼ cup fresh lemon juice
5 tablespoons Dijon mustard
¼ cup (½ stick) butter

Mustard Sauce
6 tablespoons (¾ stick) butter, melted
3 tablespoons fresh lemon juice
2 tablespoons Dijon mustard

For swordfish: Prepare barbecue grill with very hot coals. Pat fish dry. Brush with lemon juice. Spread 1 side with mustard. Dot with butter. Grill fish mustard side up until just opaque, about 20 minutes; do not turn.

For sauce: Heat butter, lemon juice and mustard in heavy small saucepan. Arrange fish mustard side down on plates. Spoon sauce over and serve.

Tomatoes Filled with Corn Pudding

The corn pudding is also very good on its own or baked in a quiche shell.

8 servings

8 medium tomatoes
  Salt and freshly ground pepper

2 eggs, room temperature
2 tablespoons all purpose flour
2 tablespoons sugar
½ teaspoon baking powder

1 cup half and half
1 cup corn kernels
  (about 4 medium ears)
2 tablespoons (¼ stick) butter,
  melted
  Minced fresh parsley

Slice tops off tomatoes and discard. Scoop out pulp and seeds. Sprinkle shells with salt and pepper. Invert onto paper towels. Drain 20 minutes.

Preheat oven to 350°F. Oil muffin tin. Beat eggs to blend in medium bowl. Mix in flour, sugar and baking powder. Blend in half and half. Stir in corn and butter. Season with salt and pepper. Spoon into tomatoes. Arrange in prepared tin. Bake until custard is puffed, lightly browned and firm to touch, about 45 minutes. Garnish with parsley and serve immediately.

For variation, chopped cooked bacon and/or grated cheese can be added to corn pudding before spooning into tomatoes.

Portuguese Sweet Bread

Makes 2 loaves

3 fresh yeast cakes
½ cup warm water (105°F to 115°F)

1 cup milk
½ cup (1 stick) butter,
  cut into pieces
2 teaspoons salt

6 eggs, room temperature
1 cup sugar
8 to 9 cups sifted all purpose flour

2 tablespoons (¼ stick) butter,
  melted

Crumble yeast cakes into large bowl. Stir in water. Let mixture stand until foamy, about 5 minutes.

Scald milk. Add butter and salt and stir until butter melts. Cool to lukewarm.

Using electric mixer, beat eggs until frothy. Add sugar and beat until creamy, about 3 minutes. Blend in milk mixture. Stir into yeast mixture. Stir in 7 cups flour 1 cup at a time; dough should be soft and pull away from sides of bowl. Turn dough out onto well-floured surface, sprinkle with 1 cup flour and knead until smooth and elastic, adding up to 1 cup more flour as necessary to prevent stickiness, about 10 minutes.

Grease large bowl. Add dough, turning to coat entire surface. Cover and let rise in warm draft-free area until doubled in volume, about 2 hours.

Punch dough down. Let rest 10 minutes. Grease two 9-inch round cake pans. Divide dough in half. Press each half into pan. Cover and let rise in warm draft-free area until doubled in volume, about 1 hour.

Preheat oven to 350°F. Bake until loaves are golden brown and sound hollow when tapped on bottom, about 30 minutes. Brush tops immediately with melted butter. Serve warm.

Strawberries on the Half Shell

Pastry baked on scallop shells forms the base for this fanciful dessert. Although the recipe serves eight, it makes 12 shells to allow for breakage. Be sure to serve the pastry shells within two hours of filling them.

8 servings

Pastry Shells
2¼ cups all purpose flour
¼ cup sugar
 1 cup (2 sticks) butter, cut into 16 pieces
 1 egg
 1 teaspoon vanilla
 4 tablespoons (about) ice water

Cream Cheese Filling
 1 cup whipping cream
 3 ounces cream cheese, room temperature

½ cup sugar
 1 tablespoon fresh lemon juice

Glaze
⅓ cup seedless raspberry preserves
 2 tablespoons Cointreau or Grand Marnier

 2 pints strawberries, hulled (halved if large)

For shells: Combine flour with sugar in large bowl. Cut in butter until mixture resembles coarse meal. Beat egg and vanilla to blend. Stir into flour mixture. Mix in water 1 tablespoon at a time, adding enough so dough just holds together. Gather into ball; shape into cylinder 1 inch in diameter. Wrap in plastic and refrigerate 1 hour.

Preheat oven to 400°F. Cut dough into 12 pieces. Roll each piece out on lightly floured surface into round about ⅛ inch thick. Press firmly onto back of ungreased 4- to 5-inch scallop shell* to within ⅛ inch of edge. Prick dough with fork. Arrange shells dough side up on baking sheet. Bake until lightly browned, about 12 minutes. Immediately remove pastry from back of shell. Place in shell and cool.

For filling: Beat cream to soft peaks. Using wooden spoon, stir cream cheese, sugar and lemon juice in large bowl until smooth. Fold in whipped cream. Cover and chill until ready to use.

For glaze: Melt preserves with liqueur in heavy small saucepan over low heat, stirring mixture constantly.

To assemble: Spoon filling into pastry bag fitted with plain tip. Pipe into shells, filling about ⅔ full. Stand strawberries in cream. Brush generously with glaze. Arrange shells on platter. Chill until ready to serve.

*If unavailable, use 4- to 5-inch tartlet pans with removable bottoms.

Concert-in-the-Park Supper

Tomato-Yogurt Soup
Onion and Olive Turnovers
Tricolored Fusilli with Shrimp and Roasted Peppers
Lemon and Cucumber Salad
Strawberries with Raspberry Sauce

Serves 4

Tomato-Yogurt Soup

6 servings

2½ pounds ripe tomatoes, peeled,
    seeded and chopped
2 cups plain yogurt
1 garlic clove, pressed
¼ teaspoon celery salt
¼ teaspoon curry powder
    or to taste

Juice of 1 lemon
Salt and freshly ground pepper
Plain yogurt and minced fresh
parsley (garnish)

Puree tomatoes in processor or blender. Add remaining ingredients except garnish
and mix until smooth. Taste and adjust seasoning. Pour into bowl, cover and
chill well. Garnish each serving with yogurt and minced parsley.

Onion and Olive Turnovers

Makes about 20

Savory Pastry
2 cups all purpose flour
½ cup (1 stick) chilled unsalted
    butter, cut into small pieces
2 egg yolks
1 teaspoon salt
5 tablespoons ice water

Béchamel Sauce
1 tablespoon butter
1 tablespoon all purpose flour
1 cup milk
    Salt and freshly ground pepper

Onion and Olive Filling
¼ cup (½ stick) butter
2½ cups sliced onion
1 teaspoon dried thyme, crumbled
1 large garlic clove, minced
½ cup chopped pitted black olives
½ teaspoon Dijon mustard
    Salt and freshly ground pepper

1 egg, beaten to blend

For pastry: Sift flour into work bowl of processor. Blend in butter, yolks and salt
using on/off turns until mixture resembles coarse meal. With machine running,
pour water through feed tube and mix until dough just comes together; do not
form ball. Gather dough into ball; flatten into disc. Refrigerate at least 30 minutes.

For béchamel: Melt butter in heavy small saucepan over medium-low heat. Whisk in flour and stir 3 minutes. Remove from heat and whisk in milk. Season with salt and pepper. Bring to boil. Reduce heat and simmer until thick, about 10 minutes.

For filling: Melt butter in heavy medium saucepan over low heat. Add onion, thyme and garlic and cook until tender and golden brown, stirring frequently, about 20 minutes. Remove from heat. Stir in béchamel sauce, olives and mustard. Season with salt and pepper. Cool completely. Adjust seasoning. Refrigerate until ready to use.

To assemble: Preheat oven to 400°F. Roll dough out on generously floured surface to thickness of ⅛ inch. Cut out circles using 4-inch cutter. Gather scraps. Refrigerate if necessary. Reroll and cut out additional circles. Mound 1 tablespoon filling in center of each circle. Brush edges with beaten egg. Fold dough over filling, pressing edges to seal. Arrange on baking sheet, spacing ½ inch apart. (*Can be prepared 1 day ahead and refrigerated.*) Brush with beaten egg. Bake until pastry is richly browned, about 25 minutes. Cool on rack. Store airtight.

Tricolored Fusilli with Shrimp and Roasted Peppers

4 servings

1 large red bell pepper
1 large green bell pepper

12 ounces mixed egg, spinach and tomato fusilli pasta
Salt and freshly ground pepper

½ cup white wine vinegar

1 tablespoon Dijon mustard
½ cup olive oil
8 ounces cooked small shrimp, shelled and deveined
2 to 3 tablespoons chopped fresh basil

Char peppers in broiler or over open flame, turning until skins blacken. Wrap in plastic bag and steam 10 minutes. Remove skin and seeds. Rinse and pat dry. Cut into fusilli-size strips.

Cook fusilli in large pot of rapidly boiling salted water until firm but still tender to bite. Drain, rinse under cool water and drain again. Sprinkle with salt and pepper. Cool to room temperature.

Blend vinegar, mustard, salt and pepper in bowl. Whisk in oil in thin stream. Add peppers, fusilli, shrimp and basil and toss well. Let stand at room temperature 2 hours before serving.

Lemon and Cucumber Salad

4 to 6 servings

2 large English hothouse cucumbers
3 tablespoons coarse salt

¼ cup fine julienne of lemon peel
¼ cup fine julienne of orange peel

⅓ cup fresh orange juice
1½ tablespoons fresh lemon juice
⅓ cup olive oil
Salt and freshly ground pepper

Halve each cucumber crosswise. Cut long grooves in skin using fork. Cut cucumber halves lengthwise. Scoop out hollow in center of each using melon ball cutter. Slice cucumbers ⅛ inch thick. Place slices in colander. Sprinkle with salt. Drain 30 minutes. Rinse in cold water; pat dry.

Blanch peels in simmering water 3 minutes. Rinse in cold water; pat dry.

Blend juices in nonaluminum bowl. Whisk in oil in thin stream. Season with salt and pepper. Mix in cucumber and peel. Refrigerate at least 2 hours.

Strawberries with Raspberry Sauce

4 servings

4 cups strawberries
3 cups raspberries
1½ tablespoons fresh lemon juice
Powdered sugar

½ cup crumbled macaroons or
amaretti (Italian macaroons)

Arrange strawberries in 1-quart jar. Puree raspberries in blender or food processor with lemon juice and sugar to taste. Press through fine sieve into same jar. Seal tightly and refrigerate.

Spoon strawberries with sauce into bowls. Top with macaroons and serve.

Simply Elegant Picnic

Three-Cheese Pastries
Vegetable-Lobster Terrine with Chive Mayonnaise
Sliced tomatoes or cherry tomatoes
Chocolate Paradise Cake with Candied Orange Rounds

Serves 8

Three-Cheese Pastries

Makes 5½ to 6 dozen

½ cup all purpose flour
¼ teaspoon salt
5 tablespoons chilled unsalted
butter, cut into ½-inch pieces
¼ cup crumbled imported goat
cheese (such as Montrachet)

¼ cup grated Gruyère cheese
¼ cup grated Cantal cheese*
2 tablespoons cold water

1 egg, beaten to blend
¼ cup finely chopped walnuts

Sift flour with salt into work bowl of processor. Cut in butter using 5 to 6 on/off turns. Blend in cheeses until mixture forms large crumbs. With machine running, pour 2 tablespoons water through feed tube and mix until dough just starts to come together; do not form ball. Gather dough into ball; flatten into disc. Wrap in plastic. Refrigerate at least 30 minutes.

Preheat oven to 375°F. Roll dough out on generously floured surface to thickness of ¼ inch, lifting dough and flouring surface and rolling pin frequently to prevent sticking. Brush off excess flour. Glaze with beaten egg. Sprinkle with walnuts, pressing gently to adhere. Cut out circles using 1-inch cutter. Arrange on baking sheet, spacing ½ inch apart. Bake until lightly browned around edges, about 12 minutes. Cool on rack. Store in airtight container.

Pastries can be prepared 1 week ahead.

*If unavailable, Emmenthal or white cheddar can be substituted.

Vegetable-Lobster Terrine with Chive Mayonnaise

For best flavor, peel turnips past tough, woody "ring" just below surface.

8 servings

Vegetable-Lobster Terrine
- 1 2-pound whole live lobster

- 12 ounces turnips, peeled and diced
- 12 ounces carrots, diced
- 12 ounces zucchini, diced
- 12 ounces green beans, trimmed and cut into ½-inch pieces

- ⅓ cup all purpose flour
- 1 cup milk
- ¼ teaspoon salt
  Pinch of cayenne pepper
- 5 eggs

Chive Mayonnaise
- 1 egg yolk, room temperature
- 2 tablespoons Dijon mustard
- 1 teaspoon white wine vinegar
  Salt and freshly ground white pepper
- ½ cup vegetable oil
- ½ cup olive oil
- 3 tablespoons snipped fresh chives

For terrine: Plunge lobster head first into large pot of boiling salted water. Cook until bright red, 8 to 10 minutes. Remove from water and cool completely. Remove meat from shells; cut into ¾-inch cubes. Set aside.

Preheat oven to 350°F. Generously butter 1½-quart terrine. Blanch vegetables separately in large pot of boiling salted water until crisp-tender. Drain, rinse under cool water and drain again. To remove excess water, stir vegetables in large dry pot over high heat for 30 seconds. Combine lobster and vegetables. Spoon into prepared terrine, packing firmly.

Sift flour into large bowl. Make well in center. Add ½ cup milk, salt and cayenne to well. Gradually incorporate flour, whisking until smooth. Gently whisk in eggs. Stir in remaining ½ cup milk. Pour batter into terrine. Tap sharply on counter to eliminate air pockets. Cover tightly with buttered foil. Set in roasting pan. Add enough water to come halfway up sides of terrine. Bring water just to boil on top of stove, then transfer to oven and bake until skewer inserted in center comes out clean, 1½ to 2 hours. Let stand at room temperature 2 hours. Chill well, about 4 hours. Before departing for picnic, run knife around sides of terrine. Invert onto surface. Slice thinly. Repack into terrine. Cover tightly.

For mayonnaise: Blend yolk, mustard, vinegar, salt and pepper in medium bowl. Gradually whisk in oils in thin stream. Stir in chives. Adjust seasoning. Spoon into jar. Cover tightly.

Unmold sliced terrine onto platter. Pass mayonnaise separately.

Chocolate Paradise Cake with Candied Orange Rounds

At its best when you marinate the orange-mint mixture for the full four days. Rock candy adds a special flavor.

8 to 10 servings

- 1 cup rock candy
- 6 oranges, peeled and cut into ¼-inch rounds
- 12 fresh mint leaves

- 8 ounces semisweet chocolate, chopped
- ½ cup crème fraîche

- 12 eggs, separated, room temperature
- 1¼ cups sugar
- ¾ cup finely ground almonds

  Pinch of cream of tartar
- ¼ cup powdered sugar

Cover bottom of 1-quart canning jar with rock candy. Top with layer of orange rounds. Add 2 mint leaves. Continue layering with remaining sugar, orange rounds and mint leaves to within ½ inch of top of jar, pressing down between each layer. Cover tightly and refrigerate 3 to 4 days.

Preheat oven to 350°F. Butter and flour 10-inch cake pan. Line pan with parchment; butter and flour paper. Line cake rack with parchment. Melt chocolate with crème fraîche in double boiler over gently simmering water. Stir until smooth.

Beat yolks and 1¼ cups sugar in large bowl using electric mixer until slowly dissolving ribbon forms when beaters are lifted. Blend in ground almonds, then melted chocolate mixture.

Using electric mixer, beat whites in large bowl with cream of tartar to soft peaks. Gradually add ¼ cup powdered sugar and beat until stiff but not dry. Gently fold ¼ cup into chocolate mixture to loosen. Fold in remaining whites. Pour into prepared pan. Bake until outer third of cake is set (top will appear cracked) but inside is still moist, 75 to 90 minutes. Run knife around edge of pan. Invert cake onto prepared rack and cool completely. Carefully peel off paper. Just before serving, garnish with candied orange rounds.

Terrific Texas Barbecue

Border Bombshell
Texas Smoky Short Ribs
Corn and Chili Custard
Orange-Jícama Salad
Pecan Fudge Tarts

Serves 2

Border Bombshell

2 servings

⅔ cup crushed ice
6 tablespoons tequila
¼ cup fruit nectar (such as passionfruit or mango)

2 tablespoons fresh lime juice
2 lime slices

Mix ice, tequila, nectar and lime juice in blender on low speed 10 to 15 seconds. Pour into 2 chilled wine glasses. Garnish each with lime slice.

Texas Smoky Short Ribs

Ribs can be cooked and sauce prepared up to three days ahead.

2 servings

2 pounds short ribs, trimmed
1 medium onion, chopped
1 bay leaf
  Salt and freshly ground pepper

2 tablespoons corn oil
1 medium celery stalk, chopped
½ small green bell pepper, seeded and chopped
1 medium garlic clove, minced
1 cup catsup

¼ cup red wine vinegar
2 tablespoons chili powder
1 teaspoon Liquid Smoke
½ teaspoon dried basil, crumbled
½ teaspoon dried oregano, crumbled
½ teaspoon ground cumin

Combine short ribs, half of onion, bay leaf and salt and pepper in large pot. Cover with cold water and bring to boil. Let boil 5 minutes, skimming foam from surface. Reduce heat, cover and simmer until ribs are tender, 1 to 1¼ hours. Drain short ribs well, reserving 1 cup cooking liquid.

Heat oil in heavy medium saucepan over medium-low heat. Add remaining onion, celery, bell pepper and garlic and cook until softened, stirring occasionally, about 10 minutes. Add reserved cooking liquid and remaining ingredients and simmer until sauce is thick, about 30 minutes.

Preheat oven to 350°F. Arrange ribs in baking dish. Spoon sauce over. Cover with foil. Bake until heated through, about 30 minutes. Serve hot.

Corn and Chili Custard

2 servings

½ cup creamed corn
½ cup grated sharp cheddar cheese
½ cup cooked rice
¼ cup cornmeal
¼ cup milk
¼ cup sliced black olives (about 7 large)
2 tablespoons chopped green onion

1 tablespoon seeded, deveined and chopped jalapeño peppers
1 tablespoon vegetable oil
1 egg, beaten to blend
½ teaspoon salt
⅛ teaspoon baking powder
1 drop hot pepper sauce

Preheat oven to 350°F. Generously grease 3-cup baking dish or ovenproof bowl. Mix all ingredients. Spoon into prepared dish. Bake until slightly puffed and lightly browned, about 30 minutes. Serve immediately.

Orange-Jícama Salad

2 servings

  Butter lettuce leaves
1 large orange, peeled and thinly sliced
1 cup julienne of peeled jícama, Jerusalem artichoke or celery root
½ cup chopped red onion

1 tablespoon fresh orange juice
1 teaspoon white wine vinegar
  Salt and freshly ground pepper
3 tablespoons olive oil
1 tablespoon minced fresh cilantro or parsley

Line plates with lettuce. Top with orange slices. Mound with jícama. Sprinkle with chopped red onion.

Blend juice, vinegar, salt and pepper in small bowl. Whisk in oil in thin stream. Spoon over salads. Garnish with minced cilantro or parsley.

Pecan Fudge Tarts

2 servings

Crust
- ³/₄ **cup all purpose flour**
- ¹/₂ **teaspoon sugar**
  Pinch of salt
- 3 **tablespoons butter,**
  cut into pieces
- 2 **tablespoons (about) ice water**

Filling
- 2 **tablespoons (¹/₄ stick) butter**
- 1¹/₂ **tablespoons unsweetened cocoa**
  powder

- ¹/₄ **cup hot water**
- 2 **tablespoons milk**
- ¹/₂ **cup sugar**
- 2 **tablespoons all purpose flour**
- ¹/₄ **teaspoon vanilla**
  Pinch of salt
- ¹/₄ **cup coarsely chopped pecans**

For crust: Combine flour, sugar and salt in bowl. Cut in butter using pastry blender or 2 knives until mixture resembles coarse meal. Using fork, stir in enough water so dough just comes together; do not overwork. Gather into ball. Wrap in plastic; chill 15 minutes.

Press dough into bottom and sides of two 4¹/₂-inch tart pans with removable bottoms. Chill until ready to bake.

For filling: Preheat oven to 375°F. Melt butter in heavy small saucepan. Remove from heat. Stir in cocoa powder until smooth. Blend in water and milk. Whisk in sugar, flour, vanilla and salt. Stir in pecans. Pour into tart shells. Bake until filling is firm, about 30 minutes. Serve at room temperature.

Tarts can be made a day ahead and kept at room temperature.

 # Cross-Country Ski Warmup

Hot Perked Apple Cider
Papagayo Black Bean Soup
Caraway-Cheddar Muffins
Soaked Salad
Backpacker Bars
Three-Nut Fudge

Serves 6 to 8

Hot Perked Apple Cider

8 servings

- 8 **cups apple cider**
- ¹/₂ **cup loosely packed light**
  brown sugar

- 10 **3-inch cinnamon sticks**
- 6 **whole cloves**

Pour cider into large percolator. Place remaining ingredients in percolator basket. Perk 10 minutes. Pour into warmed vacuum bottle. Drain cinnamon sticks in basket and pat dry. Wrap and transport to picnic; garnish each serving of cider with cinnamon stick.

Papagayo Black Bean Soup

6 to 8 servings

1 pound dried black beans
2 quarts (or more) water
5 to 6 ounces bacon, finely chopped
1 pound onions, finely chopped
2 to 3 canned serrano chilies or 1 to 1½ canned jalapeños, drained, seeded and finely chopped
2 tablespoons finely chopped garlic

1 tablespoon ground cumin
1 tablespoon dried oregano, crumbled
¼ cup water
1 tablespoon dried epazote,* crumbled (optional)
Salt
Queso fresco** or Monterey Jack cheese, crumbled

Rinse beans under hot water. Combine beans and 2 quarts water in heavy large pot. Simmer until beans are tender, stirring occasionally and adding more water as necessary to keep beans covered, about 5 hours.

Cook bacon in heavy large skillet over medium heat until light brown, stirring frequently. Add onions, 2 serrano chilies or 1 jalapeño chili and garlic. Reduce heat to low and cook until onions are soft, stirring frequently, about 10 minutes. Add onion mixture to beans. Blend in cumin and oregano. Transfer ½ cup of soup to blender or processor. Add ¼ cup water and epazote. Puree until smooth. Return mixture to soup. Simmer 30 minutes, stirring occasionally. Season with salt. Add remaining chili if desired. Turn soup into warmed vacuum bottle. Pack cheese separately for topping soup.

*A pungent herb that is available at some Latin American markets.
**A fresh cheese available at Latin American markets and some supermarkets.

Caraway-Cheddar Muffins

Makes about 12

1½ cups all purpose flour
½ cup rye flour
3 tablespoons sugar
2 teaspoons baking powder
1 teaspoon caraway seeds, ground
½ teaspoon baking soda
½ teaspoon salt

1⅔ cups finely shredded extra-sharp cheddar cheese
⅔ cup sour cream
½ cup milk
6 tablespoons vegetable oil
1 egg, room temperature
1 teaspoon Worcestershire sauce

Preheat oven to 400°F. Generously grease 2½-inch muffin cups or line with foil baking cups. Mix first 7 ingredients in large bowl. Stir in cheese. Whisk sour cream, milk, oil, egg and Worcestershire in medium bowl until smooth. Make well in center of dry ingredients. Add sour cream mixture to well; stir into dry ingredients until just blended (batter will be thick). Spoon batter into prepared cups, filling each ¾ full. Bake until muffins are golden brown and tester inserted in center comes out clean, 25 to 30 minutes. Cool 5 minutes. Turn out of pan. Serve muffins warm or cooled.

Soaked Salad

Marinate this salad for at least three hours before serving time.

8 servings

1 bunch watercress, stemmed
1 bunch spinach, stemmed and torn into bite-size pieces
1 cup loosely packed stemmed turnip greens or other greens, torn into bite-size pieces
3 large tomatoes, cut into 1-inch pieces
1½ tablespoons white wine vinegar

1½ tablespoons fresh lemon juice
½ teaspoon minced garlic
½ teaspoon salt
½ teaspoon coarsely ground pepper
¼ teaspoon sugar
9 tablespoons olive oil
1½ tablespoons minced fresh parsley
1½ tablespoons minced fresh basil
½ cup sliced mushrooms

Combine first 4 ingredients in salad bowl. Mix vinegar, lemon juice, garlic, salt, pepper and sugar in small bowl. Gradually whisk in oil. Stir in parsley and basil. Pour over salad and toss. Cover and refrigerate 3 to 6 hours. Just before serving, top with mushrooms.

Backpacker Bars

Makes 2½ dozen

1 cup (2 sticks) butter
1½ cups firmly packed light brown sugar
1 cup quick-cooking oats
1 cup whole wheat flour
1 cup all purpose flour
½ cup wheat germ

4 teaspoons grated orange peel
4 eggs, beaten to blend
2 cups whole almonds
1 cup semisweet chocolate chips
½ cup chopped dates
½ cup chopped dried apricots
½ cup shredded or flaked coconut

Preheat oven to 350°F. Cream butter with 1 cup brown sugar in large bowl until well blended. Stir in oats, flours, wheat germ and orange peel. Spread mixture evenly in bottom of 9 × 13-inch baking pan. Combine eggs, almonds, chocolate chips, dates, apricots, coconut and remaining ½ cup brown sugar in another large bowl and mix gently but thoroughly. Pour over butter mixture, spreading evenly. Bake until browned, about 30 to 35 minutes. Let cool. Cut into bars. Store in airtight container.

Three-Nut Fudge

An energy-packed sweet treat.

Makes 64 one-inch squares

¾ cup sugar
¾ cup water
1 teaspoon solid vegetable shortening
¾ cup milk

½ cup unsalted cashews
½ cup raw almonds
½ cup shelled unsalted pistachios
5 to 6 drops green food coloring

Heat sugar, water and shortening in heavy 2-quart saucepan over low heat until sugar dissolves, swirling pan occasionally. Increase heat and bring to boil. Add milk and boil until mixture is thick, 30 to 40 minutes (1 drop placed on greased pan, cooled and pinched should feel thick and tacky).

Meanwhile, blend nuts in processor until mixture resembles cornmeal, scraping down sides of bowl.

Grease 8-inch square baking pan. Remove milk mixture from heat. Blend in food coloring. Add nuts and stir until mixture stiffens slightly, 3 to 4 minutes. Pour into prepared pan, spreading evenly. Grease knife edge and mark 1-inch squares. Cool completely. Cut into squares. Store airtight in cool dry place.

🍎 *Epicurean Picnic*

Tomato Soup with Tarragon
Roast Duck and Red Grape Salad
Roquefort and Walnut Loaf
Peaches Poached with Ginger and Monbazillac Wine

Serves 4

Tomato Soup with Tarragon

4 servings

3 **fresh tarragon branches or**
 1 tablespoon dried, crumbled

1 **tablespoon olive oil**
1 **large onion, thinly sliced**
4 **large tomatoes**
 (about 2 pounds), quartered
4 **cups (or more) chicken stock,**
 preferably homemade

1 **tablespoon tomato paste**
1 **fresh thyme sprig or**
 1 teaspoon dried, crumbled
½ **bay leaf**
 Salt
 Cayenne pepper

Remove leaves from 1 tarragon branch; reserve for garnish.

Heat olive oil in heavy large saucepan over low heat. Add onion, cover and cook until translucent, stirring occasionally, about 10 minutes. Stir in tomatoes. Blend in 4 cups chicken stock, tomato paste, 2 tarragon branches and 1 tarragon stem, thyme, bay leaf, salt and cayenne. Increase heat to medium and bring to boil. Reduce heat and simmer until soup thickens, stirring occasionally, about 25 minutes. Cool to room temperature.

Puree soup in blender or processor. Strain through fine sieve to eliminate seeds if desired. (If soup is too thick, thin with more stock. If too thin, simmer to thicken.) Refrigerate.

Before packing, adjust seasoning. To serve, pour or ladle soup into bowls. Garnish with reserved tarragon leaves.

Roast Duck and Red Grape Salad

4 servings

1 **3- to 4-pound duck, trussed**
 and patted dry
 Salt and freshly ground pepper

3 **tablespoons red wine vinegar**
3 **tablespoons Cognac**
2 **tablespoons green peppercorns,**
 rinsed and drained

6 **tablespoons walnut oil**
12 **ounces red grapes**

1 **head oak leaf or red leaf lettuce**
2 **medium-size green onions, sliced**

Preheat oven to 400°F. Sprinkle duck with salt and pepper. Set on one side on rack in roasting pan; roast 10 minutes. Turn duck onto other side; roast 10 minutes. Reduce temperature to 350°F. Turn duck onto back; roast until juices run light pink when thigh is pierced with knife tip, about 20 minutes. Cool.

Remove duck meat from bones; discard skin. Slice meat thinly. Blend vinegar, Cognac and peppercorns in nonaluminum bowl. Season with salt and pepper. Whisk in oil in slow steady stream. Mix in duck and grapes. Cover tightly and let stand at room temperature at least 2 hours.

To serve, arrange lettuce leaves on plates. Mound salad in center. Spoon marinade over. Garnish with onions.

Roquefort and Walnut Loaf

The whimsical bread container keeps these sandwiches moist between home and picnic site.

4 servings

½ cup Roquefort cheese, room temperature
½ cup (1 stick) unsalted butter, room temperature
½ cup chopped walnuts

1 large, round, firm whole wheat bread, 2 to 3 days old

Puree cheese and butter in processor until smooth. Transfer to medium bowl. Fold in chopped walnuts.

Insert long serrated knife down into bread about 1 inch in from edge. Cut outline of circle all the way around, cutting to within 1 inch of bottom. Insert knife horizontally just above bottom and move knife back and forth to release bread round in one piece. Pull out bread. Slice off top of bread to form lid. Cut 2 slits in center of lid and insert decorative ribbon. Cut bread round horizontally into thin layers. Spread half of layers with cheese mixture. Top each with another layer to form sandwiches. Cover and refrigerate until cheese mixture sets.

Cut each sandwich into 8 wedges. Stack wedges in bread shell to re-form mound. Cover with lid at angle.

Peaches Poached with Ginger and Monbazillac Wine

Monbazillac is a golden, Sauternes-style wine from southwestern France.

4 servings

1 750-ml bottle sweet white wine, preferably Monbazillac
½ cup sugar
2 tablespoons chopped fresh ginger
4 large firm peaches, peeled (reserve peel)

½ teaspoon finely grated lemon peel
2 tablespoons chopped candied ginger

Cook wine, sugar and fresh ginger in heavy saucepan over low heat until sugar dissolves, swirling pan occasionally. Increase heat and bring to simmer. Add peaches and peel. Cook until peaches are tender, turning occasionally and adjusting heat so liquid is barely shaking, 10 to 15 minutes.

Transfer peaches to storage container. Strain syrup into clean saucepan. Boil until reduced to 2 cups, about 8 minutes. Cool slightly. Pour over peaches. Cover tightly and refrigerate.

To serve, set each peach in dessert dish. Spoon syrup over. Garnish with chopped candied ginger.

Weekend Grill Dinner

Black Pepper Sticks
Grilled Cornish Game Hens Mont Ventoux
Spaghetti Vinaigrette
Espresso Slush with Whipped Cream
Ruth's Madeleines

Serves 6

Black Pepper Sticks

Vary the flavor by changing the pepper to sesame seeds, poppy seeds, minced garlic or Parmesan cheese.

Makes about 12

2 cups (or more) all purpose flour
1 envelope fast-rising yeast
1 teaspoon salt
½ to 1 teaspoon coarsely cracked black pepper

¾ cup (or more) hot water (125°F to 130°F)
1 tablespoon olive oil

Additional olive oil

Combine 2 cups flour, yeast, salt and pepper in processor. With machine running, pour ¾ cup water and 1 tablespoon oil through feed tube and process until dough cleans sides of work bowl. If dough sticks to bowl, add more flour through feed tube 1 tablespoon at a time, incorporating each before adding next. If dough is dry, add water through feed tube 1 teaspoon at a time, incorporating each before adding next. Process dough until smooth and elastic, about 40 seconds. Knead on lightly floured surface 1 minute. Transfer dough to oiled bowl, turning to coat entire surface. Cover bowl. Let dough rise in warm area for 30 minutes.

Preheat oven to 450°F. Coat baking sheet with olive oil. Roll walnut-size pieces of dough into 10-inch sticks. Arrange on baking sheet, spacing 1 inch apart. Bake until brown, 10 to 15 minutes. Cool on rack before serving.

Can be prepared 1 day ahead. Recrisp in 350°F oven about 5 minutes.

Grilled Cornish Game Hens Mont Ventoux

These succulent hens are named for a charming town in Provence.

6 servings

5 1-pound Cornish game hens, halved lengthwise
⅓ cup coarse kosher salt
10 garlic cloves

¼ cup hazelnut oil or olive oil
¼ cup minced fresh herbs (such as mint, oregano, thyme, marjoram or basil)
¼ teaspoon salt
¼ teaspoon freshly ground pepper
6 thin, 5-inch-long zucchini, trimmed

6 leeks (white part only), trimmed, split lengthwise and rinsed
3 Japanese eggplants, trimmed and halved lengthwise
2 medium-size red bell peppers, quartered, cored and seeded

1½ cups feta or Montrachet cheese
¼ cup minced fresh herbs (such as mint, oregano, thyme, marjoram or basil)

Place hens in large nonaluminum bowl or baking dish. Combine ⅓ cup salt and garlic in blender. Add enough water to measure 1 quart. Blend until garlic is pureed. Pour over hens, turning to coat thoroughly. Cover and marinate in refrigerator 8 to 24 hours.

Combine oil, ¼ cup herbs, ¼ teaspoon salt and pepper in large bowl. Mix in vegetables. Let stand 1 hour.

Prepare barbecue grill. Arrange leeks around outer edge of barbecue rack.* Cook 10 minutes. Arrange remaining vegetables around outer edge of rack and cook 10 minutes. Drain game hens. Arrange skin side down in center of grill. Cook until hen legs move easily and vegetables are crisp-tender, turning hens and vegetables frequently, about 25 minutes. Cut zucchini in half lengthwise if desired.

Preheat broiler. Transfer hens and vegetables to broilerproof platter. Sprinkle with cheese. Broil until cheese melts. Sprinkle with ¼ cup herbs and serve.

*If grill will not accommodate hens and vegetables at one time, vegetables can be cooked in oven. Arrange in single layer in large baking dish. Bake in 400°F oven about 1 hour, turning occasionally.

Spaghetti Vinaigrette

Prepare the dressing and vegetables ahead of time, then just toss with the hot pasta at the last minute. Leftovers are nice cold or at room temperature.

6 servings

Garlic Dressing
1 cup olive oil
1 cup red wine vinegar
1 tablespoon minced garlic
1½ teaspoons salt
   Freshly ground pepper

1 pound thin spaghetti

12 fresh Italian plum
   tomatoes, diced
1½ cups diced red onion
1 large or 2 small bunches arugula,
   coarsely chopped
   Whole green onions (optional)

For dressing: Combine first 5 ingredients in jar. Cover and shake to blend. (*Can be prepared 1 day ahead.*)

Cook spaghetti in large pot of rapidly boiling salted water, stirring to prevent sticking, until just tender but firm to bite. Drain. Transfer spaghetti to large bowl. Mix in half of dressing. Blend in vegetables and arugula and enough of remaining dressing to coat lightly. Garnish with green onions and serve.

Espresso Slush with Whipped Cream

6 servings

7 cups freshly brewed espresso
¾ cup (or more) sugar
½ cup dark rum

1 cup whipping cream

2 teaspoons sugar
1 teaspoon vanilla
   Chocolate coffee bean candies

Combine espresso, ¾ cup sugar and rum in large bowl and stir until sugar dissolves. Taste and add more sugar if desired. Refrigerate until well chilled.

Transfer espresso mixture to ice cream maker* and process according to manufacturer's instructions. (*Can be prepared 4 hours ahead. Freeze in covered container. Let stand at room temperature for 30 minutes to soften.*)

Just before serving, whip cream to soft peaks with sugar and vanilla. Spoon espresso slush into wine glasses. Top with whipped cream and garnish with chocolate coffee bean candies.

*Can also be made in food processor. Freeze espresso mixture in ice cube trays until firm. Let stand at room temperature 30 minutes to soften slightly. Spoon half into processor and blend until slushy. Transfer to bowl. Repeat with remainder.

Ruth's Madeleines

A simple, foolproof technique for making these French classics.

Makes 3 dozen

³/₄ cup (1¹/₂ sticks) butter
2 eggs, room temperature
1 cup sugar

1 cup sifted all purpose flour
1 teaspoon vanilla

Preheat oven to 450°F. Generously butter and flour 36 madeleine molds. Melt ³/₄ cup butter in small saucepan over low heat. Cool to room temperature. Beat eggs in top of double boiler until blended. Set eggs over boiling water. Gradually add sugar, beating with wooden spoon until mixture is lukewarm. Remove from over water and continue beating until cool. Blend in flour. Mix in melted butter and vanilla. Spoon batter into prepared molds, filling ³/₄ full. Bake until light brown, about 9 minutes. Immediately remove from molds. Cool completely on racks before serving.

 # Easy Lunch at the Ballpark

**Curried Chicken Salad with Apples
    on Spiced Fruit Bread
Marinated Cucumber Salad
Orange-Coconut Delights
Tea Lemonade**

Serves 8

Curried Chicken Salad with Apples on Spiced Fruit Bread

Bread and salad are both delicious on their own but are especially good combined in a sandwich. You will have enough bread for a double recipe of the curried chicken salad.

Makes two 9 × 5-inch loaves and about 5 cups chicken salad

Spiced Fruit Bread
  2 cups warm milk (105°F to 115°F)
  2 tablespoons sugar
  1 envelope dry yeast
  2 bananas, mashed (1 cup)
  1 cup raisins
  ¹/₄ cup (¹/₂ stick) butter, melted
      Grated peel of 2 oranges
  2 tablespoons cinnamon
  1 tablespoon salt
  5 to 6 cups bread flour or
      unbleached all purpose flour

  1 egg
  1 tablespoon milk

Chicken Salad
  3 cups chopped cooked chicken

  1 large red apple, cored and
      finely diced
  ¹/₂ cup plain yogurt
  ¹/₃ cup mayonnaise
  2 tablespoons plus 2 teaspoons
      fresh lemon juice
  1 tablespoon curry powder
      or to taste
  ¹/₃ cup chopped fresh parsley
  ¹/₄ cup grated onion
      Salt and freshly ground pepper

      Crushed peanuts
      Boston lettuce leaves

For bread: Oil very large bowl and set aside. Pour ½ cup warm milk into another large bowl. Add sugar and yeast and stir until dissolved. Let stand until foamy, 5 to 10 minutes. Blend in 1½ cups warm milk, bananas, raisins, melted butter, orange peel, cinnamon and salt. Using wooden spoon, stir in flour 1 cup at a time until dough can be kneaded. Turn dough out onto floured surface and knead until smooth and elastic, about 10 to 15 minutes, adding remaining flour as necessary. Transfer dough to oiled bowl, turning to coat entire surface. Cover with damp towel. Let stand in warm area until doubled, about 1½ hours.

Grease two 9 × 5-inch loaf pans. Punch dough down and knead lightly. Divide dough in half. Shape each half into loaf and transfer to prepared pans. Cover with damp towel. Let stand in warm area until doubled, about 35 minutes.

Preheat oven to 375°F. Blend egg and remaining 1 tablespoon milk in cup. Brush tops of loaves with egg mixture to glaze. Bake until loaves sound hollow when tapped, about 50 minutes. Turn out onto racks to cool completely.

For salad: Combine chicken and apple in large bowl. Blend yogurt, mayonnaise, lemon juice and curry powder in small bowl. Add to chicken mixture and toss to coat. Stir in parsley, onion and seasoning. Cover and chill.

For sandwiches: Spread slice of bread with chicken salad. Sprinkle with peanuts. Top with lettuce and second bread slice.

Marinated Cucumber Salad

4 servings

2 cucumbers, peeled and sliced
4 green onions, chopped into
    ½-inch pieces
¼ cup red wine vinegar

1 tablespoon soy sauce
1 tablespoon vegetable oil
    Freshly ground pepper

Combine all ingredients in nonaluminum medium bowl. Cover and refrigerate several hours or overnight. Serve salad chilled.

Orange-Coconut Delights

Makes 60 unbaked cookies

1 12-ounce box vanilla wafers
1 cup chopped walnuts
    (about 4 ounces)
1 16-ounce box powdered sugar
½ cup (1 stick) butter,
    room temperature

1 6-ounce can frozen orange juice
    concentrate, thawed
2 cups shredded coconut

Combine vanilla wafers and walnuts in processor and chop finely. Mix powdered sugar, butter and orange juice concentrate in medium bowl. Add to cookie crumbs and process until blended. Form mixture into 1-inch balls. Roll in coconut. Serve at room temperature. Store cookies in refrigerator.

Tea Lemonade

Makes about 10 cups

5 tablespoons tea leaves
2 quarts boiling water

3/4 cup cold water
3/4 cup granulated or
    turbinado sugar

3/4 cup fresh lemon juice
Mint sprigs

Preheat teapot with hot tap water; let stand for a few minutes. Discard water and add tea to pot. Pour boiling water over tea. Cover and let brew for 5 to 7 minutes. Strain.

Combine cold water and sugar in medium saucepan and bring to boil over high heat. Reduce heat to medium and simmer 3 minutes.

Mix tea, sugar syrup and lemon juice. Cool, then chill. Pour over ice. Garnish with mint sprigs.

 # Country-House Barbecue

Virgin Islands Piña Colada
Creamy Carrot Soup
Barbecued Flank Steak
Mixed Vegetable Grill
Basil and Sage Bread
Lemon-Almond Squares

Serves 4

Virgin Islands Piña Colada

For a nonalcoholic version of this classic drink, omit rum and brandy and add 1/4 teaspoon vanilla.

4 servings

4 cups ice cubes
1 cup pineapple juice
3/4 cup dark rum
1/2 cup coconut cream
1/4 cup brandy

4 fresh pineapple wedges
Mint leaves
Freshly grated nutmeg

Mix first 5 ingredients in blender until slushy. Pour into tall glasses. Garnish with pineapple, mint and nutmeg.

Creamy Carrot Soup

This versatile soup is also refreshing when served chilled.

4 servings

2¾ cups chicken stock
1 pound carrots, peeled and sliced
1 medium onion, cut into 8 wedges
1½ teaspoons curry powder
½ teaspoon dried thyme, crumbled
½ teaspoon freshly grated nutmeg
1 garlic clove, pressed
1 bay leaf

1 cup milk
3 ounces cream cheese, cubed, room temperature
1 teaspoon grated orange peel (optional)
Salt
Toasted sliced almonds
Minced fresh parsley

Combine stock, carrots, onion, curry powder, thyme, nutmeg, garlic and bay leaf in large saucepan over medium-low heat. Cover and simmer until vegetables are tender, about 15 minutes. Discard bay leaf. Puree soup in blender or processor in 4 batches. (*Can be prepared 8 hours ahead, covered and refrigerated.*) Return soup to saucepan. Stir in milk. Warm gently over low heat until heated through. Add cream cheese and stir until melted. Blend in orange peel if desired. Season with salt. Ladle into bowls. Garnish with nuts and parsley. Serve immediately.

Barbecued Flank Steak

4 servings

¾ cup vegetable oil
⅓ cup soy sauce
3 tablespoons honey
3 tablespoons red wine vinegar

2 teaspoons ground ginger
1 green onion, chopped
1 large garlic clove, crushed
1 1½-pound flank steak, trimmed

Combine first 7 ingredients. Place steak in large glass baking dish and pour marinade over. Cover and refrigerate overnight, turning steak twice.

Prepare barbecue. Grill steak to desired doneness, 4 to 5 minutes per side for rare. Slice into thin strips across grain and serve.

Mixed Vegetable Grill

4 servings

2 artichokes
½ medium lemon

2 medium onions, halved lengthwise

4 ears corn, unhusked
2 Japanese eggplants, halved lengthwise

2 red bell peppers, halved lengthwise, cored and seeded
2 medium zucchini, halved lengthwise
4 large fresh boletus, oyster or shiitake mushrooms*

½ cup olive oil

Break stems off artichokes. Cook artichokes with lemon in boiling salted water until bottoms are tender, 20 to 30 minutes. Halve artichokes lengthwise. Remove innermost leaves. Discard chokes and lemon half.

Prepare barbecue grill, heating coals until white. Arrange onion halves cut side down on grill and cook 5 minutes.

Place corn directly on coals. Arrange all other vegetables cut side down on grill and cook until crisp-tender, turning once, 5 to 7 minutes.

Husk corn. Divide vegetables among plates. Drizzle with oil and serve.

*If fresh are unavailable, dried can be substituted. Soak in warm water to rehydrate.

Basil and Sage Bread

Makes 2 baguettes

1 envelope dry yeast
1 cup warm water (105°F to 115°F)
5½ cups (or more) all purpose flour

¼ cup olive oil
4 teaspoons dried basil, crumbled

¼ teaspoon dried sage, crumbled
½ cup dry white wine
1¾ teaspoons salt
¼ teaspoon freshly ground pepper
½ cup warm water (105°F to 115°F)

Sprinkle yeast over 1 cup water in bowl of heavy-duty electric mixer; stir to dissolve. Let stand 5 minutes. Thoroughly mix in 1½ cups flour. Sprinkle ½ cup flour over dough. Cover with towel. Let rise in warm draft-free area until doubled in volume, about 1½ hours.

Heat oil in heavy small skillet over low heat. Add basil and sage and stir until aromatic, about 1 minute. Cool. Blend 1 cup flour, oil mixture, wine, salt and pepper into dough, using dough hook. Slowly add remaining ½ cup water. Stir in 2½ cups flour ½ cup at a time. Knead dough in mixer until smooth and resilient, about 10 minutes, adding more flour if sticky.

Grease large bowl. Add dough, turning to coat entire surface. Cover bowl. Let dough rise in warm draft-free area until doubled, about 1¼ hours.

Grease two baking sheets. Punch dough down. Divide in half. Form each piece into 14-inch-long loaf. Place on prepared sheets seam side down. Let rise in warm draft-free area until almost doubled, about 1 hour.

Preheat oven to 400°F. Slash tops of loaves with sharp knife. Bake until breads sound hollow when tapped on bottom, about 50 minutes. Cool on wire racks before serving.

Lemon-Almond Squares

Makes about 16

Crust
1 cup all purpose flour
¼ cup powdered sugar
Pinch of salt
½ cup (1 stick) unsalted butter

Lemon-Almond Filling
2 eggs, room temperature
½ cup sugar

1 3½-ounce roll almond paste, crumbled
2 tablespoons fresh lemon juice
1 teaspoon grated lemon peel
2 tablespoons all purpose flour

Powdered sugar

For crust: Preheat oven to 350°F. Mix flour, sugar and salt in medium bowl. Cut in butter until mixture holds together when pressed. Pat into bottom of 9-inch square baking dish. Bake until light brown, about 15 minutes.

Meanwhile, prepare filling: Using electric mixer, beat eggs and ½ cup sugar until thick, pale yellow and slowly dissolving ribbon forms when beaters are lifted. Add almond paste and beat until smooth. Mix in lemon juice, lemon peel and all purpose flour.

Pour filling into crust. Bake until filling is firm but not brown, 17 to 20 minutes. Cool in pan. (*Can be prepared 1 day ahead. Wrap tightly.*) Dust with powdered sugar. To serve, cut into squares using knife dipped in hot water.

Casual Poolside Cookout

Pistarckle Punch
Cheddar Burgers with Onion Hamburger Rolls
New Potatoes in Sean's Creamy Savory Dressing
Tomatoes in Herb Vinaigrette
Caramel Praline Sundaes

Serves 8

Pistarckle Punch

Makes 12 cups

4 cups water
2 cups sugar

2½ cups fresh orange juice
2½ cups guava nectar
1½ cups minced fresh pineapple
1¼ cups fresh lemon juice
1 tablespoon finely grated
orange peel

2 teaspoons finely grated
lemon peel
2 tablespoons grenadine
Ice cubes
Lemon slices
Mint leaves

Cook water and sugar in heavy medium saucepan over low heat until sugar dissolves, swirling pan occasionally. Increase heat and bring to boil. Cool.

Blend orange juice, guava nectar, pineapple, lemon juice and peels in large pitcher. Stir in sugar syrup and grenadine. Pour into large ice-filled glasses. Garnish with lemon and mint.

Cheddar Burgers

Makes 8

8 ounces sharp cheddar cheese,
chilled and cut into 1-inch cubes
2 pounds lean beef, cut into
1-inch cubes and chilled
8 ounces beef fat, cut into
1-inch cubes and chilled
¼ cup ice water *or*

1 egg, beaten to blend
3 teaspoons Worcestershire sauce
1½ teaspoons salt
Freshly ground pepper

Onion Hamburger Rolls
(see following recipe)

Finely chop cheese in processor. Remove from work bowl. Combine ⅓ of beef with ⅓ of fat and chop finely, about 20 seconds. Add ⅓ of cheese, 4 teaspoons water, 1 teaspoon Worcestershire, ½ teaspoon salt and pinch of pepper. Mix until cheese is evenly distributed, about 5 seconds. Remove from work bowl. Repeat with remaining ingredients in 2 more batches. Gently form mixture into 8 patties.

Prepare barbecue grill; oil rack. Cook patties to desired degree of doneness 4 to 6 inches from heat, turning once. Serve with rolls.

Onion Hamburger Rolls

Makes 10

1 egg
½ teaspoon salt
1 medium onion, quartered
¼ cup (½ stick) unsalted butter

¾ cup warm water (105°F to 115°F)
1 envelope dry yeast
1 teaspoon sugar

3 cups (or more) bread flour
1 egg, room temperature
2 tablespoons instant nonfat
   dry milk powder
1¼ teaspoons salt

Oil large bowl. Mix egg and salt in processor 2 seconds. Remove and set aside for glaze; do not clean work bowl. Finely chop onion. Melt butter in 8-inch skillet over medium-low heat. Add onion and cook until very soft but not brown, 8 to 10 minutes. Remove from heat and cool to lukewarm.

Pour warm water into cup. Stir in yeast and sugar. Let mixture stand until foamy, about 10 minutes.

Combine 3 cups flour, egg, milk powder, salt and all but 4 tablespoons sautéed onion in processor work bowl. With machine running, pour yeast mixture through feed tube and mix until dough is uniformly moist and elastic and cleans sides of work bowl, about 40 seconds, adding more flour 1 teaspoon at a time if dough is sticky. Transfer dough to prepared bowl, turning to coat entire surface. Cover with damp towel. Let dough stand in warm draft-free area until doubled in volume, about 1 hour.

Grease baking sheet. Punch dough down. Turn out onto lightly floured surface and divide into 10 pieces. Shape each piece into ball, then flatten into circle 3¼ inches in diameter and ¾ inch thick. Arrange 1½ to 2 inches apart on prepared baking sheet, pressing to flatten. Brush rolls with egg glaze. Gently press about 1 teaspoon reserved sautéed onion onto each. Drape loosely with oiled plastic wrap. Let stand in warm area until almost doubled, about 45 minutes.

Position rack in center of oven and preheat to 375°F. Bake rolls until golden, about 20 minutes. Transfer to racks to cool. Slice rolls horizontally.

For variation, dough can be braided into loaf. Divide dough into thirds. Roll each into smooth rope 15 inches long; braid together. Pinch ends and tuck under. Brush with egg glaze. Press sautéed onion gently into surface. Transfer to greased baking sheet. Cover and let rise in warm draft-free area until doubled in volume, about 45 minutes. Bake until golden, about 35 minutes. Transfer to rack and cool completely.

New Potatoes in Sean's Creamy Savory Dressing

8 servings

1¾ pounds tiny new potatoes

1 egg, room temperature
⅔ cup corn oil
¼ cup cider vinegar
1½ teaspoons Dijon mustard
1½ teaspoons minced fresh
   summer savory

1 teaspoon salt
½ teaspoon sugar
¼ teaspoon freshly ground white
   pepper

Boil potatoes until just tender. Cool. (*Can be prepared 1 day ahead and refrigerated.*) Peel; slice thinly on diagonal.

Whisk egg in small bowl to blend. Slowly whisk in oil in thin stream. Blend in remaining ingredients. Arrange potatoes on platter. Drizzle lightly with dressing. Serve at room temperature, passing remaining dressing.

Tomatoes in Herb Vinaigrette

8 servings

½ cup fresh parsley leaves
1 tablespoon fresh tarragon leaves
1 medium garlic clove
1 egg, room temperature
½ cup vegetable oil
3 tablespoons red wine vinegar

½ teaspoon salt
Pinch of sugar
Freshly ground pepper
2 pounds tomatoes, cored and thinly sliced

Place parsley and tarragon in processor work bowl. With machine running, drop garlic through feed tube and mince finely. Add egg, oil, vinegar, salt, sugar and pepper and mix 5 seconds. Arrange tomatoes in serving bowl or on rimmed platter. Pour dressing over. Adjust seasoning.
Can be prepared 2 hours ahead.

Caramel Praline Sundaes

8 servings

Pecan Praline
⅔ cup sugar
8 teaspoons water
⅔ cup pecans

Caramel Butter Sauce
1¼ cups sugar
⅓ cup water
⅛ teaspoon salt
Pinch of cream of tartar

⅓ cup whipping cream
½ cup (1 stick) unsalted butter, cut into 8 pieces

Maple Whipped Cream
1 cup chilled whipping cream
2 tablespoons sugar
1 teaspoon maple flavoring

1½ quarts rich vanilla ice cream

For praline: Lightly oil baking sheet. Combine sugar and water in heavy 2-quart saucepan. Place over high heat and cook, without stirring, until mixture just begins to color. Add pecans and continue cooking, gently swirling pan constantly, until mixture registers 320°F on candy thermometer. Immediately pour onto prepared baking sheet, spreading nuts out with wooden spoon. Cool.

Carefully break praline into 2-inch pieces. Chop coarsely in processor using on/off turns. (*Praline can be wrapped and frozen up to 6 months.*)

For sauce: Combine sugar, water, salt and cream of tartar in heavy 2-quart saucepan. Cook over high heat, swirling pan, until mixture turns medium brown, about 5 minutes; *do not stir*. Remove from heat. Pour cream on top; *do not stir*. Mixture will foam and bubble. When bubbling subsides, stir mixture. Dot top with butter and let melt, then beat vigorously with wooden spoon. (*Can be refrigerated up to 4 weeks.*)

For maple cream: Whip cream and sugar in large bowl of electric mixer until soft peaks form. Add maple and beat until just slightly stiffer.

To serve: Reheat caramel sauce in top of double boiler set over gently simmering water. Scoop ice cream into individual sundae glasses or bowls. Pass pecan praline, warm caramel butter sauce and maple whipped cream.

Warm-Weather Tête à Tête

Caribbean Wine Coolers
Iced Tomato and Watercress Soup
Poached Salmon with Avocado Mayonnaise
Summer Compote
Praline Cookies

Serves 2

Caribbean Wine Coolers

2 servings

1 teaspoon superfine sugar
2 dashes Angostura bitters
2 tablespoons fresh lime juice
2 tablespoons fresh orange juice
4 teaspoons Cognac
Cracked ice

1 cup dry white wine
Club soda
2 dashes grenadine
2 lime slices
2 strawberries

Stir sugar and bitters in small pitcher until sugar dissolves. Mix in juices and Cognac. Divide mixture between 2 tall glasses filled with cracked ice. Stir in white wine. Top up with club soda. Blend in grenadine. Garnish each with lime slice and strawberry and serve.

Iced Tomato and Watercress Soup

2 servings

2 tablespoons (¼ stick) butter
1 medium leek, chopped (white part only)
¼ cup chopped onion
1 garlic clove, minced
1½ cups chicken stock
1 cup peeled cubed potato
2 large ripe tomatoes, peeled, seeded and chopped

1 cup firmly packed watercress leaves
1 tablespoon minced fresh parsley
Pinch of sugar

½ cup whipping cream
Salt and freshly ground pepper
Watercress sprigs

Melt butter in heavy medium saucepan over low heat. Add leek, onion and garlic. Cover and cook until vegetables are tender, stirring occasionally, about 10 minutes. Add stock, potato and tomatoes. Increase heat and bring to boil. Reduce heat and simmer until potato is tender, 10 to 15 minutes. Add watercress leaves, parsley and sugar and simmer 10 minutes. Cool to room temperature.

Puree soup in blender until smooth. Blend in cream. Season generously with salt and pepper. Refrigerate until chilled. *(Can be prepared 1 day ahead.)* Ladle soup into bowls. Garnish with watercress sprigs and serve.

Poached Salmon with Avocado Mayonnaise

2 servings

2 6-ounce salmon fillets, about ¹/₂ inch thick, skinned
1 cup dry white wine
1 cup water
1 thin onion slice
1 parsley sprig

Avocado Mayonnaise
¹/₂ medium avocado
1 small shallot, minced

2 tablespoons fresh lemon juice
1 tablespoon fresh orange juice
1 teaspoon Dijon mustard
1 egg yolk, room temperature
²/₃ cup vegetable oil
Salt and freshly ground white pepper

2 lemon slices
2 avocado slices

Combine salmon, wine, water, onion and parsley in 8-inch skillet. Bring to simmer over low heat and cook 5 minutes per ¹/₂ inch thickness of fish, basting occasionally. Cool completely in liquid. Transfer salmon to plates using slotted spatula. Cover with plastic wrap and chill. *(Can be prepared 1 day ahead.)*

For mayonnaise: Mix avocado and shallot in processor until very smooth. Blend in juices, mustard and yolk. With machine running, add oil through feed tube in thin stream. Season with salt and pepper. *(Can be prepared 2 to 3 hours ahead, covered and chilled.)*

Top salmon with mayonnaise. Garnish with lemon and avocado and serve.

Summer Compote

2 servings

¹/₃ cup sugar
3 tablespoons ruby Port

2 nectarines, peeled and thinly sliced

1 cup cantaloupe balls
¹/₂ cup raspberries

Cook sugar and Port in heavy small saucepan over low heat until sugar dissolves, swirling pan occasionally. Increase heat and boil 30 to 45 seconds.

Combine nectarines, cantaloupe and raspberries in medium bowl. Pour syrup over and stir gently. Cover and refrigerate until chilled. Divide between 2 dessert bowls and serve.

Praline Cookies

Makes 3 dozen

1 cup all purpose flour
¹/₄ teaspoon baking soda
¹/₄ teaspoon salt
¹/₈ teaspoon mace
¹/₂ cup sugar

¹/₃ cup butter, melted and cooled
¹/₄ cup molasses
1 egg
¹/₂ teaspoon vanilla
1 cup chopped pecans or walnuts

Preheat oven to 350°F. Grease baking sheets. Sift together first 4 ingredients. Combine sugar, butter, molasses, egg and vanilla and beat well. Add dry ingredients and mix thoroughly. Stir in nuts. Drop by scant teaspoonfuls onto prepared sheets, spacing 2 inches apart. Bake until lightly golden, about 10 minutes. Immediately transfer cookies to wire racks and let cool.

Easy-but-Elegant Tailgate Party

Zesty Gazpacho with Clams
Pesto Cheesecake
    and/or
Romano-Ricotta Cheesecake
Tossed green salad
Sesame breadsticks
Brandied Fruit

Serves 10 to 12

Zesty Gazpacho with Clams

Makes about 11 cups

1 6½-ounce can minced clams
3½ to 3¾ cups tomato juice
½ cup catsup
2 tablespoons fresh lemon juice
1 tablespoon prepared horseradish
1 tablespoon Worcestershire sauce
  Freshly ground pepper

1 large unpeeled cucumber, seeded and cut into 1-inch pieces
1 medium-size green bell pepper, cored, seeded and cut into 1-inch pieces

4 medium celery stalks, peeled and cut into 1-inch pieces
6 large green onions, trimmed and cut into 1-inch pieces
4 large tomatoes, peeled, seeded and quartered

1 medium avocado, peeled, pitted and cut into ⅛-inch cubes

Drain liquid from clams into 4-cup measure (reserve clams for garnish). Add enough tomato juice to make 4 cups liquid. Transfer to 3-quart mixing bowl. Add catsup, lemon juice, horseradish, Worcestershire and pepper.

Combine half of cucumber, green pepper, celery and green onion in processor and chop finely using 6 to 7 on/off turns; *do not overprocess.* Add to tomato juice mixture. Repeat with remaining half of vegetables. Place half of tomato in work bowl and chop coarsely using on/off turns. Add to tomato juice mixture. Repeat with remaining tomato. Stir to blend.

Cover gazpacho and refrigerate several hours or overnight. Taste and adjust seasoning. Garnish each serving with minced clams and diced avocado.

Pesto Cheesecake

12 servings

1½ tablespoons butter (for pan)
¼ cup fine breadcrumbs,
  lightly toasted
¼ cup freshly grated
  Parmesan cheese

2½ cups fresh basil leaves
½ cup parsley sprigs, stemmed
¼ cup olive oil
½ teaspoon salt
1 garlic clove, halved

1 pound fresh whole-milk ricotta
  cheese*, room temperature
1 pound cream cheese,
  room temperature
8 ounces freshly grated
  Parmesan cheese
4 eggs
⅓ cup lightly toasted pine nuts
  Basil leaves (garnish)

Preheat oven to 325°F. Butter bottom and sides of 9-inch springform pan. Mix breadcrumbs and ¼ cup Parmesan. Sprinkle mixture into pan, turning to coat completely. Refrigerate.

Mix basil leaves, parsley, oil, salt and garlic in blender until smooth paste forms, about 2 minutes, scraping sides occasionally. Transfer to large bowl. Add ricotta, cream cheese and 8 ounces Parmesan to blender and mix until smooth, about 2 minutes. Mix in eggs. Blend in basil mixture. Pour into prepared pan. Sprinkle with pine nuts. Set pan on baking sheet. Bake 1¼ hours. Turn oven off and cool cheesecake about 1 hour with door ajar. Transfer to rack. Remove springform. Cool to room temperature before serving. Garnish with basil.

*Skim-milk ricotta can be substituted.

Romano-Ricotta Cheesecake

12 servings

1 tablespoon unsalted butter
  (for pan)
1 cup fine breadcrumbs,
  lightly toasted
⅓ cup freshly grated Romano or
  Parmesan cheese
5 tablespoons unsalted butter,
  melted

1 pound fresh whole-milk ricotta
  cheese,* room temperature
1 pound cream cheese,
  room temperature

6 ounces freshly grated pecorino
  Romano or Asiago cheese
4 eggs
¼ cup half and half
3 tablespoons snipped fresh chives
1 tablespoon minced fresh
  rosemary or 1 to 1½ teaspoons
  dried, crumbled
1 small garlic clove, minced

Preheat oven to 350°F. Butter 9-inch springform pan. Mix breadcrumbs, ⅓ cup Romano and melted butter. Press mixture firmly onto bottom and sides of pan. Bake until crust is set, about 8 to 10 minutes. Let cool.

Preheat oven to 325°F. Mix ricotta, cream cheese and 6 ounces Romano in blender or processor. Add eggs, half and half, 2 tablespoons chives, rosemary and garlic and mix until smooth. Pour into prepared pan. Sprinkle top with remaining chives. Set pan on baking sheet. Bake 1¼ hours. Turn oven off and cool cheesecake about 1 hour with door ajar. Transfer cheesecake to rack. Remove sides of pan. Cool to room temperature before serving.

*Skim-milk ricotta can be substituted; use whipping cream instead of half and half.

Brandied Fruit

12 servings

3 cups dried fruit (apricots, raisins, figs and/or dates) cut into 1-inch pieces

³/₄ cup sugar
³/₄ cup water
4 or 5 whole cloves
³/₄ cup Cognac or brandy

6 cups fresh fruit (apples, pears, melon, oranges, tangerines, kumquats, pineapple) cut into 1-inch pieces

Place dried fruit in bowl. Cover with boiling water and let soak 10 minutes.

Heat sugar, ³/₄ cup water and cloves in heavy small saucepan over low heat, swirling pan occasionally, until sugar dissolves. Increase heat to medium and boil until syrupy, about 5 minutes. Remove cloves. Add Cognac to pan. Cool syrup to lukewarm.

Drain dried fruit. Transfer to serving bowl. Add fresh fruit. Stir in syrup. Refrigerate overnight, stirring occasionally. Let stand at room temperature for 1 hour before serving.

Rustic Italian Picnic

Gorgonzola-Pistachio Loaf
Zesty Tomato Sandwiches
Crisp Orange Cookies
Fresh fruit

Serves 4

Gorgonzola-Pistachio Loaf

In this menu, you may wish to omit the crackers and serve the cheese loaf alongside the tomato sandwiches.

Makes one 8 × 4-inch loaf

1 pound cream cheese, room temperature
8 ounces Gorgonzola cheese, room temperature
1 cup (2 sticks) unsalted butter, room temperature

1 cup chopped fresh parsley
1 cup shelled pistachios

Fresh parsley sprigs
Shelled pistachios
Crackers

Moisten two 18-inch cheesecloth squares. Line 8 × 4-inch loaf pan with cheesecloth, draping excess over sides. Combine cream cheese, Gorgonzola and butter in large bowl and blend with rubber spatula. Spread ¹/₃ of cheese mixture into prepared pan. Sprinkle with chopped parsley. Cover with half of remaining cheese mixture. Sprinkle with 1 cup pistachios. Cover with remaining cheese mixture. Fold ends of cloth over and press down lightly. Chill until firm, about 1 hour.

Invert onto serving plate. Carefully remove cheesecloth. Garnish with parsley sprigs and pistachios. Serve cheese loaf at room temperature with crackers.

Zesty Tomato Sandwiches

4 servings

1 large loaf Italian or French bread
4 large ripe tomatoes, thinly sliced
1 small sweet red onion, thinly sliced

Olive oil or homemade mayonnaise
Salt and freshly ground pepper

Cut bread in half lengthwise. Pull out half of interior. Cut loaf crosswise into 8 pieces. Arrange bread slices, tomatoes and onions on large platter. Pass olive oil and salt and pepper separately.

Can be assembled 1 day ahead, wrapped tightly in foil and refrigerated.

Crisp Orange Cookies (Biscotti all'Arancio)

These slightly sweet rum-laced cookies have a crackerlike texture.

Makes about 28

2½ cups unbleached all purpose flour
¼ cup (½ stick) unsalted butter, melted and cooled
½ cup cold water
5 tablespoons sugar
1 extra-large egg yolk
2 tablespoons grated orange peel
1 tablespoon olive oil

1 tablespoon light rum
3 drops orange extract
Pinch of salt

1 extra-large egg, beaten to blend (glaze)
2 tablespoons (¼ stick) unsalted butter, melted

Arrange flour in mound on work surface and make well in center. Add ¼ cup melted butter, water, 2 tablespoons sugar, yolk, orange peel, oil, rum, orange extract and salt to well and blend with fork. Gradually draw all but ¼ cup flour from inner edge of well into center. Gather dough together and knead in remaining flour until smooth, about 1 minute. Wrap in floured towel. Refrigerate 2 hours.

Position rack in center of oven and preheat to 325°F. Lightly butter 2 baking sheets. Roll dough out on lightly floured surface to thickness of ¼ inch. Cut dough into 2 × 4-inch strips using scalloped pastry wheel. Place cookies on prepared sheets, spacing ½ inch apart. Pierce each several times with fork. Brush with egg glaze. Bake until light brown, about 25 minutes.

Brush remaining 2 tablespoons melted butter over hot cookies. Sprinkle with remaining 3 tablespoons sugar. Return to oven 5 minutes. Cool completely on rack. Store in airtight container.

Lunch on the Riviera

Cold Melon Soup
Veal and Chicken Loaf with Arugula Sauce
Carrot and Red Pepper Slaw
Herbed Prosciutto Flatbread
Shirley's Chocolate Madeleines

Serves 6 to 8

Cold Melon Soup

Serve in crystal or glass stemware for added elegance.

6 to 8 servings

3 cups coarsely chopped cantaloupe
3 cups coarsely chopped honeydew melon
2 cups fresh orange juice
1/3 cup fresh lime juice

3 tablespoons honey or to taste (depending on sweetness of melons)
2 cups brut Champagne or dry white wine
Fresh mint leaves

Finely chop half of cantaloupe and honeydew and set aside. Puree remaining melon in batches with orange and lime juices and honey in processor or blender. Pour into large bowl. Stir in Champagne or wine and reserved melon. Cover and chill several hours. Garnish each serving with mint leaves.

Veal and Chicken Loaf with Arugula Sauce

Before measuring flour, sift into dry measuring cup and sweep level.

8 to 10 servings

2 cups chicken stock
1/2 cup (1 stick) unsalted butter
3 teaspoons salt
2 cups sifted unbleached all purpose flour
4 eggs, room temperature
4 egg whites, room temperature

1 pound veal, trimmed, cut into 1/2-inch pieces and chilled
1 pound chicken breast meat, skinned, trimmed, cut into 1/2-inch pieces and chilled

3 medium leeks, white part only, coarsely chopped
1 teaspoon dried thyme, crumbled
1/2 teaspoon freshly grated nutmeg
1/4 teaspoon cayenne pepper
1 cup chilled whipping cream

3 to 4 beefsteak tomatoes, sliced into rounds
Arugula Sauce*
Arugula leaves

Combine stock, butter and 2 teaspoons salt in heavy medium saucepan and heat until butter melts and liquid just comes to boil. Remove from heat. Whisk in flour all at once. Set pan over low heat and stir until dough forms ball and film forms on bottom of pan, about 5 minutes. Remove from heat. Cool 7 minutes.

Beat in eggs one at a time. Add egg whites and beat until shiny and smooth, about 5 minutes. Cover dough; keep at room temperature until ready to use.

Position rack in center of oven and preheat to 350°F. Generously butter 12-cup loaf pan. Coarsely chop veal in processor using 4 to 5 on/off turns. Add chicken and coarsely chop using 4 to 5 on/off turns. Add remaining salt, leeks, thyme, nutmeg and cayenne and blend 1 minute. With machine running, add cream through feed tube in thin stream, stopping to scrape down sides of bowl. Add meat mixture to dough and blend well. Spoon mixture into prepared pan. Smooth top using back of metal spoon dipped in cold water. Tap pan on surface several times to eliminate air bubbles. Wrap pan tightly in buttered foil. Set in shallow roasting pan. Add enough boiling water to come ¾ up sides of loaf pan. Bake until tester inserted in center comes out *almost* clean or until instant-reading thermometer inserted in center registers 180°F to 190°F, about 2 hours. Remove from water bath. Carefully peel off foil. Cool loaf to room temperature. Wrap well. Refrigerate at least 12 hours.

To unmold, run thin sharp knife around edge of pan. Set bottom in hot water for 2 minutes. Invert loaf onto work surface. Turn upright and cut into thin slices. Spoon some of sauce onto platter. Alternate loaf and tomato slices on platter. Garnish with arugula leaves. Pass remaining sauce separately.

*Arugula Sauce

This can be prepared up to four hours ahead. Do not refrigerate any longer, or sauce may become bitter.

Makes about 3 cups

3 quarts water	⅓ cup white wine vinegar
Salt	1 tablespoon Dijon mustard
4 firmly packed cups trimmed arugula (about 4 bunches)	1 teaspoon salt
	1 cup olive oil
2 eggs, room temperature	1 cup corn oil
1 egg yolk, room temperature	

Bring water to boil in heavy large saucepan. Stir in salt. Remove pan from heat. Stir in arugula. Drain immediately. Plunge into large bowl of ice water. Let cool completely. Drain well; squeeze dry. Coarsely chop arugula. Transfer to processor. Add eggs, yolk, vinegar, mustard and 1 teaspoon salt and blend 1 minute, stopping to scrape down sides of bowl. With machine running, add oils through feed tube in thin stream. Adjust seasoning. Transfer sauce to bowl. Cover and refrigerate up to 4 hours.

Carrot and Red Pepper Slaw

6 to 8 servings

½ cup balsamic vinegar	2 medium-size red bell peppers, finely diced
¼ cup Dijon mustard	
3 egg yolks	5 green onions, thinly sliced
½ teaspoon salt	1½ pounds carrots, peeled and coarsely shredded
Freshly ground pepper	
1 cup corn oil	Savoy cabbage leaves
1 cup olive oil	

Blend vinegar, mustard, yolks, salt and pepper in processor 1 minute. With machine running, pour oils through feed tube in thin stream. Transfer dressing to bowl. Adjust seasoning. Cover and chill until ready to use.

Set aside 1 tablespoon each bell peppers and green onions. Combine remaining bell peppers, green onions and carrots in large bowl. Toss with about

⅔ of dressing. Season salad generously with pepper and toss again. Arrange cabbage leaves on platter. Spoon salad into leaves. Sprinkle with reserved bell peppers and green onions. Serve immediately or refrigerate until ready to use. Pass remaining salad dressing separately.

Herbed Prosciutto Flatbread

6 to 8 servings

1 envelope dry yeast
2 cups warm water
   (105°F to 115°F)
5 cups unbleached all purpose flour
2 teaspoons salt

1 4-ounce piece prosciutto,
   cut into ¼-inch cubes

¼ cup cornmeal
   Freshly ground pepper
½ cup minced mixed fresh
   rosemary and oregano
2 tablespoons olive oil

Sprinkle yeast over water in large bowl and let stand until dissolved. Stir to blend. Let stand until foamy, about 10 minutes. Whisk in 2 cups flour and salt. Cover and chill batter 12 hours.

Stir 2 cups flour into batter. Sprinkle ½ cup flour onto work surface. Turn dough out onto surface. Sprinkle dough with remaining ½ cup flour. Knead until flour is incorporated, about 5 minutes. Pat dough into 12-inch circle. Sprinkle prosciutto over dough. Gather into ball and knead until prosciutto is evenly distributed, about 5 minutes. Generously oil large bowl. Add dough to bowl, turning to coat entire surface. Cover loosely. Refrigerate 4 hours.

Position rack in upper third of oven and preheat to 475°F. Sprinkle 12 × 18-inch jelly roll pan or baking sheet with cornmeal. Generously flour work surface and hands. Turn dough out onto surface. Pat dough into 12 × 18-inch rectangle. Transfer to prepared pan; stretch and pat to fit. Sprinkle with pepper, then herbs, pressing gently. Drizzle with olive oil. Bake until golden, about 20 minutes. Let cool in pan 10 minutes. Serve hot.

Can be prepared 2 days ahead. Wrap tightly and store at room temperature. Just before serving, brush generously with olive oil. Grill or broil until crisp.

Shirley's Chocolate Madeleines

These fudgy madeleines can be baked in batches without your having to cool the pan between each batch.

Makes about 2½ dozen

4 ounces semisweet chocolate,
   coarsely chopped
¾ cup (1½ sticks) unsalted butter,
   melted and cooled
1¼ cups sifted cake flour
½ teaspoon baking powder

¼ teaspoon salt
3 eggs, room temperature
1 teaspoon vanilla
⅔ cup sugar
   Powdered sugar

Preheat oven to 350°F. Butter 30 madeleine molds. Melt chocolate in top of double boiler set over hot water. Stir in butter. Mix together flour, baking powder and salt. Beat eggs in large bowl of electric mixer until light and lemon colored; add vanilla. Gradually add sugar, beating constantly at high speed 5 minutes. Reduce speed to medium and beat until mixture has quadrupled in volume, about 5 minutes. Gently fold in flour mixture, then chocolate. Place 1 tablespoon batter in center of each mold. Bake exactly 12 minutes. (Madeleines should be moist and fudgy in center.) Cool on rack. Dust with powdered sugar before serving.

Can be prepared 1 day ahead. Store in airtight container.

Home-on-the-Range Dinner for 8

Raised Meat Pie
Medallions of Smoked Rabbit
Barbecued Rabbit
Composed Summer Salad
Sugar-glazed Strawberries
Almond Gingersnaps

Serves 8

Raised Meat Pie

Lamb can be substituted for the game.

8 servings

8 ounces veal stew meat, cut into ³/₈-inch cubes
8 ounces ham, cut into ³/₈-inch cubes
1 small onion, minced
   Freshly grated nutmeg
   Salt and freshly ground pepper
   Hot Water Pastry*
12 ounces cooked game (elk, pheasant, deer), cut into ¹/₂-inch cubes

3 hard-cooked eggs, ends cut flat
1 egg beaten with 1 teaspoon water (glaze)
1 tablespoon unflavored gelatin
2 cups canned beef consommé

Preheat oven to 400°F. Generously grease 9¹/₄-inch pâté en croûte mold or 7- or 8-inch cake pan with removable bottom. Mix veal, ham, onion, nutmeg, salt and pepper in large bowl. Roll ²/₃ of warm pastry out to thickness of ¹/₈ inch, smoothing any cracks with warm water. (Wrap remaining pastry in foil to keep warm.) Line prepared mold with pastry. Trim and finish edges. Arrange half of meat mixture in crust. Cover with half of game. Press 1-inch-deep trench down center of filling. Line eggs up in trench lengthwise. Cover with remaining game, then remaining meat mixture, pressing lightly to smooth.

Roll remaining pastry out ¹/₈ inch thick. Drape pastry over dish. Trim off excess dough and reserve. Brush edges with water and crimp to seal. Cut ¹/₂-inch hole in center of top to allow steam to escape. Reroll trimmings; cut into leaves. Brush underside with water and arrange decoratively atop pie. Brush surface with egg glaze. Bake 30 minutes, cutting top hole open if necessary. Reduce oven temperature to 325°F. Brush pie with glaze again. Continue baking until thermometer inserted into center of mixture registers 160°F, about 1 hour.

Meanwhile, soften gelatin in ¹/₄ cup consommé. Bring remaining 1³/₄ cups consommé to simmer in small saucepan. Add gelatin and stir until dissolved. Remove from heat.

Set pie on rack. Place funnel in vent hole. Slowly pour in consommé mixture until pie is filled, tilting to distribute evenly. Repeat every 20 minutes with re-

*Top to bottom:
Tricolored Fusilli with
Shrimp and Roasted
Peppers; Lemon and
Cucumber Salad; Onion
and Olive Turnovers*

Clockwise from far right:
Tomato Soup with
Tarragon; Roquefort and
Walnut Loaf; Roast Duck
and Red Grape Salad; Peach
Poached in Ginger and
Monbazillac Wine

Irwin Horowitz

Clockwise from right:
Three-Cheese Pastries;
Vegetable-Lobster Terrine
with Chive Mayonnaise;
Chocolate Paradise Cake with
Candied Orange Rounds

Irwin Horowitz

Left to right: Grilled Pork Fajitas with Chiles Chipotles; Marinated Vegetable Salad in a Jar; Chilled White Bean and Buttermilk Soup

Paul Elson

Clockwise from right:
Frozen Daiquiri; Pistarckle
Punch; Caribbean Wine
Cooler; Virgin Islands Piña
Colada; Jamaica Farewell

Greek-style Salad

maining consommé, melting consommé if necessary. Cool pie to room temperature. Refrigerate overnight. Bring to room temperature and unmold before serving.
Pie can be prepared up to 3 days ahead.

*Hot Water Pastry

3½ cups unbleached all purpose flour
1½ teaspoons salt

14 tablespoons water
4 ounces lard, coarsely chopped

Combine flour and salt in large bowl and make well in center. Simmer water and lard until lard melts, then bring to boil. Pour into well. Gradually draw flour from inner edge into center until all flour is incorporated, using wooden spoon. Knead dough until smooth, about 3 minutes. *Use while still warm.*

Medallions of Smoked Rabbit

Have the butcher cut up two rabbits: Use fillets for this recipe and save legs and thighs for Barbecued Rabbit (see next recipe).

8 servings

1¾ cups milk
1 cup fresh breadcrumbs
1½ pounds skinned and
  boned chicken breast,
  cut into 2-inch pieces
⅓ cup Crème Fraîche*
1 egg
1½ teaspoons salt
1 teaspoon sugar
¼ teaspoon freshly ground pepper

¼ cup coarse-grained mustard
1¾ cups (3½ sticks) unsalted
  butter, melted

4 cups coarse fresh breadcrumbs
4 teaspoons tarragon mustard
4 rabbit fillets

30 charcoal briquettes
6 tablespoons clarified butter
1½ cups mesquite chips, soaked
  in water to cover 1 hour
  and drained

Stir milk and 1 cup breadcrumbs in heavy 2½-quart saucepan over medium-high heat until mixture holds shape on spoon, about 9 minutes. Cover and cool to lukewarm. Puree chicken, crème fraîche, egg, salt, sugar and pepper in processor. Add milk mixture and process using on/off turns until just blended. Refrigerate 1 hour. (*Can be prepared 2 days ahead.*)

Whisk coarse-grained mustard into ¾ cup melted butter in small bowl. Combine coarse breadcrumbs with remaining 1 cup melted butter and tarragon mustard in pie plate. Brush rabbit with butter-mustard mixture. Coat each fillet with 6 tablespoons chicken puree, using rubber spatula. Cover generously with breadcrumbs. (*Can be prepared several hours ahead and refrigerated.*)

Arrange briquettes in barbecue and heat until white. Warm clarified butter in heavy large skillet over medium-high heat. Brown rabbit well on all sides, about 5 minutes total. Push briquettes to sides of barbecue. Place 9 × 13-inch disposable aluminum pan in center. Fill with boiling water. Distribute mesquite chips over coals. Grease grill and place rabbit on grill over drip pan. Cover and smoke until firm, about 15 minutes. Cut into 1-inch slices. Serve warm.

*Crème Fraîche

Makes about 1½ cups

1½ cups whipping cream

1½ tablespoons buttermilk

Heat cream to 90°F. Pour into jar. Stir in buttermilk. Cover and let stand at room temperature until thickened, about 24 hours. Stir and refrigerate.
Can be refrigerated up to 2 weeks.

Barbecued Rabbit

Grill with the Medallions of Smoked Rabbit (see previous recipe) or save for another meal.

8 servings

Legs, with thighs attached, from 2 rabbits
¼ cup fresh lemon juice
¾ cup olive oil

2 tablespoons snipped fresh chives
2 teaspoons coarse-grained mustard
Freshly ground pepper

Place rabbit in nonaluminum pan. Whisk lemon juice into oil in thin stream. Add remaining ingredients. Pour over rabbit. Marinate in refrigerator overnight, turning occasionally.

Prepare barbecue. Drain rabbit. Grill until juices run clear when rabbit is pricked in thickest portion, turning occasionally, about 15 minutes on each side. Serve warm or at room temperature.

Composed Summer Salad

Use two or three types of lettuce in this artfully arranged salad.

8 servings

Vinaigrette Gelée
  1 **13-ounce can red or clear consommé madrilène***
  2 **tablespoons red wine vinegar**

Salad
  30 **snow peas, cut diagonally into ¾-inch slices**
  24 **baby carrots, peeled and stems trimmed to 1 inch**

  2 **heads lettuce (such as red leaf, butter, Boston), separated into leaves and chilled**

  2 **cups whole spinach leaves, stems trimmed to 1 inch**
  1 **bunch watercress, trimmed**
  ¼ **cup walnut oil**
  1 **pound fresh chanterelles or other mushrooms, cut into ½-inch pieces**
  ¾ **cup walnut halves**
  24 **radishes (with stems)**

For vinaigrette: Melt consommé in small saucepan over low heat. Stir in vinegar. Pour into 8 × 8-inch dish. Refrigerate until firm, about 3 hours. (*Can be prepared 2 days ahead.*)

For salad: Bring large saucepan of salted water to boil. Blanch snow peas 10 seconds. Remove with slotted spoon. Rinse and drain. Blanch carrots until crisp-tender. Rinse and drain.

Arrange lettuce, spinach and watercress on flat platter. Mound snow peas in center. Arrange carrots around rim of platter. Heat walnut oil in heavy large skillet over medium-high heat. Add mushrooms and sauté until browned, about 5 minutes. Stir in walnuts and sauté until hot. Spoon around snow peas. Place radishes around rim of platter. Break up vinaigrette gelée with fork and spoon atop salad. Serve immediately.

*Consommé madrilène is available at specialty foods stores and some markets.

Sugar-glazed Strawberries

Plump strawberries dipped in syrup make a beautiful dessert. At high altitude bring the syrup to 260°F.

8 servings

2 cups sugar
1 cup water

2 pints extra-large strawberries with stems

Line baking sheet with aluminum foil; butter foil. Heat sugar and water in heavy 1-quart saucepan over low heat, swirling pan occasionally, until sugar dissolves. Increase heat to medium-high and boil until syrup registers 300°F (hard-crack

stage) on candy thermometer. Reduce heat to very low. Working quickly, skewer 1 berry and dip into syrup, leaving leaves and stems exposed. Lift from syrup with swirling motion to remove excess. Slide onto prepared sheet using fork or spatula. Repeat with remaining berries. Let glaze harden before serving.
Can be prepared 1 hour ahead.

Almond Gingersnaps

The dough for these crisp cookies can be made ahead and refrigerated or frozen. Bake fresh batches as needed.

Makes about 9 dozen

3½ cups all purpose flour
1 cup sliced blanched almonds, lightly toasted
1 cup sugar
1 tablespoon ground ginger
2 teaspoons cinnamon
2 teaspoons ground cloves

1 teaspoon baking soda
1 cup (2 sticks) unsalted butter, room temperature, cut into ¼-inch pieces
½ cup dark molasses
Water (optional)

Combine first 7 ingredients in large bowl. Mix in butter and molasses using wooden spoon. If dough does not stick together when pinched, add water 1 tablespoon at a time to bind. (*Dough can also be made in electric mixer with dough hook.*) Form into three 1 × 3 × 6-inch bars. Wrap with waxed paper. Refrigerate until firm, about 4 hours. (*Can be made ahead and refrigerated 5 days or frozen 2 months. Thaw frozen dough overnight in refrigerator.*)

Preheat oven to 325°F. Cut dough into ⅛-inch slices. Arrange on baking sheet, spacing ½ inch apart. Bake until darkened, 10 to 12 minutes. Cool cookies on rack. Store in airtight container.

 Sunbelt Barbecue

Jamaica Farewell
Mexican Deviled Eggs
Beer-Barbecued Chicken
Brown Rice and Vegetable Salad
Jalapeño Corn Muffins
Mimi's Molasses Cookies

Serves 4

Jamaica Farewell

4 servings

Cracked ice
1 cup fresh orange juice
¾ cup tequila

½ cup Tía María
3 to 4 tablespoons fresh lime juice
4 orange slices

Fill cocktail shaker with cracked ice. Add all ingredients except orange slices. Shake until frosted. Strain into tall glasses filled with cracked ice. Garnish with orange and serve.

Mexican Deviled Eggs

Makes 8 hors d'oeuvres

4 hard-cooked eggs
¼ cup grated sharp cheddar cheese
2 tablespoons mayonnaise
2 tablespoons salsa
(medium-hot to hot)

1 tablespoon chopped green onion
1½ teaspoons sour cream
⅛ teaspoon freshly ground pepper

Slice eggs in half lengthwise. Transfer yolks to medium bowl. Add remaining ingredients and mix thoroughly with fork. Mound mixture into whites. Refrigerate before serving.

Beer-Barbecued Chicken

A family picnic favorite served either hot or cold.

4 servings

1 cup (2 sticks) butter or margarine
1 3-pound chicken, cut up

1 14-ounce bottle barbecue sauce
1 cup beer

Preheat oven to 350°F. Melt ½ cup butter or margarine in 9 × 13-inch pan. Add chicken; turn to coat. Bake 30 minutes.

   Meanwhile, melt remaining butter with barbecue sauce and beer in medium saucepan over medium-high heat. Bring to boil, stirring constantly. Remove from heat and set aside.

   Preheat broiler or prepare barbecue grill. Dip chicken in sauce. Arrange skin side down on rack over broiler pan or on grill. Cook, turning and basting frequently with sauce, until chicken is browned and tests done, about 10 to 20 minutes for broiler or about 30 minutes for barbecue. Dip chicken in sauce again. Transfer to platter and serve. Pass any remaining sauce separately.

Brown Rice and Vegetable Salad

4 to 6 servings

Lemon Herb Dressing
1 8-ounce carton plain yogurt
¼ cup fresh lemon juice
3 tablespoons olive oil
¼ teaspoon dried
   marjoram, crumbled
¼ teaspoon dried thyme, crumbled
¼ teaspoon garlic powder
¼ teaspoon freshly ground pepper

4 cups cooked brown rice
2 medium tomatoes, chopped, or
   15 cherry tomatoes, halved
2 small zucchini, cut into
   ¼-inch cubes (about 1¼ cups)

1 red or green bell pepper, cored,
   seeded and cut into ¼-inch cubes
   (about 1 cup)
2 celery stalks, cut into
   ¼-inch cubes (about 1 cup)
2 carrots, cut into ¼-inch cubes
   (about 1 cup)
1 10-ounce package frozen
   peas, thawed
1 8¾-ounce can corn
   kernels, drained
¾ cup thinly sliced green onion
   (green part only)
¾ to 1 cup diced pepperoni

For dressing: Combine all ingredients in bowl and mix thoroughly. Refrigerate until ready to use.

Mix remaining ingredients in large bowl. Pour dressing over. Toss salad lightly and serve.

Jalapeño Corn Muffins

Serve these hot with butter.

Makes 12

1 cup yellow cornmeal
3/4 cup all purpose flour
2 tablespoons sugar (optional)
2 teaspoons baking powder
3/4 teaspoon salt

1 cup milk
1/4 cup (1/2 stick) butter, melted
1 egg, beaten to blend
1 generous tablespoon jalapeños en escabeche, pureed

Preheat oven to 400°F. Grease 12 muffin cups. Blend first 5 ingredients in medium bowl. Combine remaining ingredients and add to dry ingredients, mixing well. Spoon batter into prepared cups. Bake until muffins are light brown, about 25 minutes. Cool in pan 5 minutes, then turn out of pan and serve.

*Available at Latin American markets and some supermarkets.

Mimi's Molasses Cookies

Makes about 50

1 cup plus 3 tablespoons solid vegetable shortening, room temperature
1 1/4 cups sugar
1/4 cup molasses
1 egg

2 1/2 cups all purpose flour
2 teaspoons baking soda
1 teaspoon cinnamon
1 teaspoon ground ginger
3/4 teaspoon ground cloves

Preheat oven to 350°F. Grease large baking sheets. Beat shortening, 1 cup sugar, molasses and egg in large bowl using electric mixer. Mix flour, baking soda, cinnamon, ginger and cloves in medium bowl. Add to shortening mixture in 3 batches, blending well after each addition. Roll dough into walnut-size pieces. Roll pieces in remaining sugar. Transfer to prepared baking sheets; press flat with spatula. Bake until crisp and golden, 10 to 12 minutes. Serve warm.

Sophisticated Grill Supper

Frozen Daiquiris
Mixed Grill of Fish with Chardonnay Cream Sauce
Bread Knots
Two-Lettuce Salad with Walnut Vinaigrette
Peaches with Lemon and Brandy

Serves 8

Frozen Daiquiris

Prepare two batches to serve eight.

4 servings

2 cups crushed ice
¾ cup light rum
¼ cup fresh lime juice

¼ cup Triple Sec
2 teaspoons superfine sugar
4 lime slices

Mix all ingredients except lime slices in blender until slushy. Pour into large stemmed glasses. Garnish with lime.

Mixed Grill of Fish with Chardonnay Cream Sauce

8 servings

1½ pounds tuna steaks
1½ pounds swordfish steaks
1½ pounds red snapper fillets
½ cup olive oil
10 fresh thyme sprigs or
   1 tablespoon dried, crumbled
10 fresh rosemary sprigs or

1 tablespoon dried, crumbled
¼ cup minced fresh parsley
¼ cup minced green onions

Rosemary and thyme sprigs (garnish)
Chardonnay Cream Sauce*

Arrange fish in single layer in nonaluminum dish. Drizzle with oil. Top with thyme, rosemary, minced parsley and green onions. Cover and refrigerate 4 to 12 hours, turning fish occasionally.

Preheat grill or broiler. Cook fish until just opaque, turning once, about 9 minutes per every inch of thickness. Arrange on platter and garnish with rosemary and thyme. Serve immediately, passing sauce separately.

*Chardonnay Cream Sauce

Makes about 2¼ cups

3 tablespoons unsalted butter	1½ bay leaves
3 tablespoons olive oil	1½ tablespoons black peppercorns
3 carrots, chopped	1½ pounds fish bones
1 medium onion, chopped	1½ 750-ml bottles
1½ celery stalks, chopped	California Chardonnay
15 fresh thyme sprigs or	
1½ tablespoons dried, crumbled	3 cups whipping cream
15 fresh tarragon sprigs or	3 tablespoons butter,
1½ tablespoons dried, crumbled	room temperature
¾ cup minced fresh parsley	Salt and freshly ground pepper

Melt 3 tablespoons butter with oil in heavy large saucepan over medium-low heat. Add carrots, onion, celery, herbs and peppercorns. Cook until vegetables are soft, stirring occasionally, about 10 minutes. Add fish bones. Stir until fish turns opaque, about 3 minutes. Add wine. Cover and simmer 20 minutes.

Strain stock through fine sieve into heavy medium saucepan. Simmer until reduced to ½ cup. (*Can be prepared 1 day ahead and refrigerated.*) Add cream to stock and simmer until reduced to 2¼ cups. Just before serving, whisk 3 tablespoons butter into sauce. Season with salt and pepper.

Bread Knots

Attractive rolls to serve with entrée or salad.

Makes 20

2 envelopes dry yeast	2 teaspoons salt
1 tablespoon sugar	3½ cups all purpose flour
1½ cups warm water	
(105°F to 115°F)	1 egg beaten with 1 tablespoon
¼ cup olive oil	water (glaze)

Lightly oil baking sheets. Sprinkle yeast and sugar over ¼ cup warm water in large bowl. Stir to dissolve. Let stand until foamy, about 5 minutes. Add oil and beat 2 minutes using wooden spoon. Stir in salt and ½ cup warm water. Alternately stir in 3 cups flour (1 cup at a time) and remaining ¾ cup warm water, beating until dough is soft and sticky.

Sprinkle remaining ½ cup flour on work surface. Turn dough out and knead until springy and flour is absorbed, about 3 minutes. Cover dough and let stand 5 minutes. Shape dough into 20-inch cylinder. Cut into 20 pieces. Let stand 4 minutes. Using palm of hand, roll each piece into cylinder. Tie into knot. Arrange on prepared sheets, spacing 1 inch apart. Cover and let stand in warm draft-free area until starting to rise, 20 to 30 minutes.

Preheat oven to 300°F. Brush knots with glaze. Bake until golden, 30 to 35 minutes. Serve bread knots warm or at room temperature.

Two-Lettuce Salad with Walnut Vinaigrette

8 servings

8 ounces bronze leaf lettuce	1 cup walnuts, toasted
8 ounces butter lettuce	and chopped
1 cup sliced radishes	Walnut Vinaigrette*
½ cup minced fresh parsley	

Tear lettuce into bite-size pieces. Combine with radishes and parsley in salad bowl. Add nuts, and vinaigrette to taste; toss well. Serve immediately.

*Walnut Vinaigrette

Makes 1 cup

¼ cup tarragon wine vinegar
1 teaspoon Dijon mustard
Salt and freshly ground pepper

½ cup vegetable oil
(preferably safflower)
¼ cup walnut oil

Combine vinegar, mustard, salt and pepper in blender or processor. With machine running, slowly pour both oils through feed tube.

Peaches with Lemon and Brandy

10 servings

2½ cups water
1⅓ cups sugar
4 lemons (unpeeled),
very thinly sliced
10 large peaches, peeled
¼ cup brandy

Clotted cream or
vanilla ice cream

Combine water and sugar in heavy 3-quart saucepan. Cook over low heat, swirling pan occasionally, until sugar dissolves. Increase heat and boil 1 minute. Add lemons and simmer 10 minutes. Add peaches and cook until tender, 7 to 8 minutes. Transfer peaches to bowl using slotted spoon. Continue cooking syrup until reduced by half, about 15 minutes. Cool syrup, then stir in brandy. Pour over peaches. (*Can be prepared 1 day ahead, covered and refrigerated. Bring to room temperature.*) Serve peaches with clotted cream.

🍒 Pan-Asian Picnic

Summer Lumpia with Sweet Sauce
Indonesian Beef Ribs with Sambal Bajak
Thai Tea
Empress Melon Bowl
Fortune cookies or Chinese almond cookies

Serves 2

Summer Lumpia with Sweet Sauce

A Philippine variation of the Chinese egg roll. Any leftover meats can be substituted for chicken.

2 servings

Lumpia
1 small onion, finely chopped
1 large garlic clove, minced
3 tablespoons minced Smithfield ham (or other deep-smoked ham)
1/4 teaspoon minced fresh ginger
6 water chestnuts, diced
1/2 cup thinly sliced bok choy (Chinese cabbage)
1/4 cup fresh bean sprouts
2 tablespoons diced celery
2 ounces medium shrimp, cooked, shelled, deveined and chopped
2 green onions, minced
2 tablespoons diced cooked chicken, turkey or duck

1 1/2 teaspoons Japanese soy sauce
1 tablespoon vegetable oil (or more)
Salt and freshly ground pepper

Sweet Sauce
1/3 cup degreased chicken stock
2 tablespoons Japanese soy sauce
2 teaspoons firmly packed brown sugar
2 garlic cloves, minced

6 large romaine or Bibb lettuce leaves, washed, drained and patted dry

For lumpia: Combine onion, garlic, ham and ginger in small bowl. Mix water chestnuts, bok choy, sprouts and celery in medium bowl. Combine shrimp, onion, chicken and soy sauce in another bowl and blend thoroughly.

Heat 1 tablespoon vegetable oil in wok or large skillet over high heat. Add onion mixture and stir-fry about 30 seconds. Add water chestnut mixture and stir-fry 1 minute, adding more oil if necessary. Add shrimp mixture and stir-fry another 30 seconds. Season to taste with salt and pepper. Transfer mixture to colander and drain. Let cool. Pack lumpia into container. Cover and refrigerate for up to 2 days.

For sauce: Combine all ingredients in small saucepan over medium-high heat and bring to boil. Let cool at room temperature. Transfer to jar with tight-fitting lid and refrigerate up to 1 week (or freeze several months).

To serve: Mound lumpia on serving platter and surround with lettuce leaves. Spoon lumpia into lettuce, roll up and dip in sauce.

Indonesian Beef Ribs with Sambal Bajak

2 servings

Beef Ribs

2 pounds beef back ribs (preferably from standing rib roast), cut crosswise into thirds and trimmed of all fat
1 garlic clove
¼ cup Japanese soy sauce
3 tablespoons Tamarind Liquid (see following recipe)
1½ tablespoons white vinegar
1 tablespoon firmly packed brown sugar
1 tablespoon vegetable oil
1 teaspoon minced fresh ginger
1 teaspoon shrimp paste (terasi)* or oyster sauce
1 teaspoon ground coriander
¼ teaspoon ground cumin
⅛ teaspoon cayenne pepper (optional)

Sambal Bajak

4 medium-hot to hot dried red chilies,** rinsed, stemmed and seeded
1 small onion, chopped
3 large garlic cloves

2 tablespoons vegetable oil
½ cup Tamarind Liquid
1 teaspoon shrimp paste (terasi) or oyster sauce
½ teaspoon firmly packed brown sugar
⅛ teaspoon salt
1 tablespoon fresh lemon juice

Banana or lemon leaves (optional garnish)

For ribs: Place ribs in shallow bowl. Combine remaining ingredients in processor or blender and puree. Pour over ribs, turning to coat evenly. Cover and marinate in refrigerator about 24 hours.

For sambal bajak: Puree chilies, onion and garlic in processor or blender.

Heat oil in small nonaluminum saucepan over medium-low heat. Add chili mixture and sauté, stirring frequently, about 3 minutes. Add next 4 ingredients and simmer about 15 minutes, stirring frequently (do not let mixture burn). Transfer to container and let cool. Stir in lemon juice and refrigerate.

To barbecue: Heat coals until gray ash forms. Spread into single layer and let burn about 30 minutes. Set grill 4 inches above coals. Arrange ribs on grill and cook until deeply browned and crisp, about 6 minutes per side.

To broil: Position rack 4 inches from heat source and preheat broiler. Pour 1 cup water into broiler pan. Arrange ribs on rack set over pan. Broil until deeply browned and crisp, about 6 minutes per side.

To serve, arrange banana or lemon leaves on serving platter and top with ribs. Accompany with individual bowls of sambal bajak for dipping.

*Available at Indonesian, oriental or Mexican markets. Wrap airtight; store at room temperature up to 1 year.
**Mild chilies can be substituted.

Tamarind Liquid

Makes about 1 cup

2 ounces dried tamarind pulp*   **1 cup boiling water**

Combine pulp and water in small bowl and let soak about 1 hour. Transfer to strainer set over bowl and drain, pressing with back of wooden spoon to extract as much liquid as possible. Discard any remaining pulp. Pour liquid into container. Cover and refrigerate up to 1 week or freeze up to 3 months.

*Available at Indonesian, oriental or Mexican markets.

Thai Tea (Nam Cha)

The two varieties of tea leaves grown in Thailand are red and black. Thai tea is brewed strong to accommodate the traditional addition of milk. When added to the red, a rich brick color results. When black tea is diluted with milk and becomes a muddy brown, Thais say that it is "Chao Phya water," named for the fast-flowing waters of the country's largest river.

Makes 4 cups

4 cups cold water
7 tablespoons red or black Thai tea leaves

4 generous teaspoons (or more to taste) sweetened condensed milk

Bring water to rapid boil in medium saucepan over high heat. Meanwhile, fit paper coffee filter into 5- to 6-inch diameter strainer. Set strainer over top of 1½-quart measure. Place tea leaves in lined strainer. Quickly pour water over tea leaves in steady stream, then stir thoroughly. Brew tea 2 minutes. Discard leaves and filter. Pour tea into 4 tall glasses. Stir 1 generous teaspoon milk into each. Serve immediately.

For iced tea, let cool to lukewarm. Fill each glass with crushed ice to 2 inches from top. Pour tea over ice. Spoon milk over and serve.

Empress Melon Bowl

Pungent Chinese rose wine is the traditional flavoring for this fruit dessert. The melon and papaya mixture is also delicious with the subtle orange taste of Grand Marnier, which is a good deal easier to find.

2 servings

2 cups melon balls (watermelon, Persian, crenshaw, casaba or cantaloupe)
1 papaya, peeled, seeded and cubed

Grand Marnier
2 tablespoons minced crystallized ginger

Mix melon and papaya in medium bowl. Add Grand Marnier to taste. Cover and refrigerate until chilled. Just before serving, spoon into dishes and sprinkle with crystallized ginger.

 # *Midsummer's Eve Patio Buffet*

Sausage and White Bean Pâté with Tomato Sauce
Gorgonzola with Madeira
Marinated Lamb Salad
Roasted Pepper Salad
Peach Bombe with Boysenberry Sauce
Butterballs

Serves 12

Sausage and White Bean Pâté with Tomato Sauce

Serve hot or cold with crackers and assorted thinly sliced breads.

12 servings

2 cups (16 ounces) dried white beans

1 ham hock
10 peppercorns
1 medium onion, quartered
1 celery stalk
1 bay leaf
4 parsley sprigs
1 teaspoon minced garlic
1 teaspoon salt

3 egg yolks
2/3 cup fine dry breadcrumbs
1/2 cup freshly grated Parmesan or Romano cheese
1/4 cup whipping cream
1/4 cup capers, rinsed and drained
1 to 2 teaspoons minced garlic
Freshly grated nutmeg
Salt and freshly ground pepper

3 egg whites

1 1-pound eggplant, peeled and coarsely grated
1/2 teaspoon salt

1 pound sweet Italian sausage, casings removed

2 cups minced onion
3 tablespoons minced fresh basil or 1 teaspoon dried, crumbled
2 teaspoons fresh lemon juice
1/2 teaspoon salt
Freshly ground white pepper

1 pound sliced bacon
Freshly grated Parmesan cheese (optional)

Tomato Sauce
4 cups strained fresh tomato puree
3/4 cup minced green onion
1/2 cup minced fresh parsley
1/4 cup minced fresh basil or 2 teaspoons dried, crumbled
2 to 4 garlic cloves, minced
2 teaspoons fresh lemon or lime juice
Salt and freshly ground white pepper

Sliced olives, lemon peel, paprika and lemon slices

Soak beans in water in large saucepan about 3 to 4 hours or overnight, discarding any beans that float to surface.

Add ham hock, peppercorns, onion, celery, bay leaf, parsley, garlic and salt and simmer over low heat until beans are tender, about 3 hours.

Drain beans well. Transfer to processor in batches and puree. Measure 3 cups puree. Pour into large bowl. Add egg yolks, breadcrumbs, cheese, cream, capers, garlic, nutmeg, salt and pepper and blend thoroughly.

Beat egg whites in medium bowl until stiff. Gently fold 1/3 of whites into puree mixture, blending thoroughly. Gently fold in remaining whites.

Place eggplant in colander and sprinkle with salt. Let drain 30 minutes. Rinse eggplant lightly; squeeze dry with towel. Measure 1 cup and set aside.

Sauté sausage in large skillet over medium heat until browned, breaking up finely with fork, about 15 minutes. Remove sausage from skillet using slotted spoon and drain on paper towels. Transfer to processor and chop finely.

Discard all but 2 tablespoons fat from skillet. Add onion to same skillet and cook until browned. Stir in eggplant and basil and cook 2 to 3 minutes. Season with lemon juice, salt and pepper. Remove from heat and set aside.

Preheat oven to 400°F. Line a 1½-quart terrine or soufflé dish with single layer of bacon slices, allowing them to hang over sides of terrine. Arrange layer of bean mixture over bacon. Add layer of sausage mixture and continue alternating mixtures until terrine is almost filled, finishing with bean puree.* Sprinkle with Parmesan if desired. Fold bacon slices over top to completely enclose pâté. Cover with terrine lid or wrap carefully in aluminum foil.

Set dish in large baking pan. Add enough boiling water to come halfway up sides of dish. Bake until set, about 45 minutes. Remove dish from water bath and let pâté stand at room temperature until cool. Refrigerate overnight (pâté will not be firm until completely chilled).**

For tomato sauce: Combine all ingredients in jar with tight-fitting lid and shake well. Taste and adjust seasoning. Refrigerate until ready to use. (*Can be made 2 to 3 days ahead, or several weeks ahead and frozen.*)

To serve, remove bacon from top of pâté and invert pâté onto platter. Discard bacon slices. Garnish top with olives, lemon peel and paprika. Surround with lemon slices. Serve with tomato sauce.

*Use excess to form small pâté. Bake pâté according to recipe directions, omitting bacon slices.
**Pâté can be frozen up to 2 weeks. If freezing, unmold when chilled but do not remove bacon slices. Wrap pâté tightly in freezer paper. Transfer to refrigerator 2 to 3 days before serving.

Gorgonzola with Madeira

Excellent either as a cheese course or hors d'oeuvre. Serve with crackers or crusty French bread and apple slices.

12 servings

8 ounces Gorgonzola or bleu cheese, room temperature
½ cup (1 stick) unsalted butter, room temperature
1 tablespoon Madeira

Green grapes and sliced nectarines (garnish)

Cream first 3 ingredients in medium bowl until well blended. Pack cheese mixture into mold. Refrigerate until firm. (*Gorgonzola with Madeira can be prepared 2 days ahead to this point and refrigerated, or 1 week ahead and frozen.*)

To serve, invert mold onto platter and discard plastic wrap. Garnish with grapes and sliced nectarines.

Marinated Lamb Salad

After marinating, lamb can be frozen up to one month.

12 servings

Marinade
1½ cups olive oil or peanut oil
1 cup minced fresh parsley
½ cup dry vermouth
8 green onions, minced
6 tablespoons minced fresh mint
4 to 6 tablespoons fresh lemon or lime juice or to taste
2 to 3 tablespoons minced garlic
2 tablespoons Grand Marnier
1 tablespoon dried rosemary, crumbled
Salt and freshly ground pepper
1 5- to 6-pound leg of lamb, boned, trimmed and cut into 1½ × ½-inch cubes

1 tablespoon olive oil or peanut oil
4 cups chopped onion

5 to 6 kiwi, thinly sliced (reserve 1 or 2 slices for garnish)

5 tablespoons minced cilantro leaves
3 to 6 whole green chilies, deveined, seeded and shredded
3 to 6 tablespoons capers, rinsed and drained
1 cup roasted cashews
1 cup minced fresh parsley
1 6-ounce can water chestnuts, drained and thinly sliced
¼ to ½ cup fresh mint leaves, chopped
¼ to ½ cup watercress leaves
½ cup toasted sesame seeds (optional)
4 to 6 tablespoons fresh lemon juice or to taste
Salt and freshly ground pepper

Combine first 9 ingredients with salt and pepper in large mixing bowl. Add lamb, tossing to coat. Cover and chill 1 to 2 days; turn once or twice each day.

Heat 1 tablespoon oil in large skillet over medium-high heat. Add onion and cook until browned, being careful not to burn. Remove with slotted spoon.

Drain lamb. Stir-fry in small batches in same skillet over high heat until just pink. *Do not overcook; test by cutting one piece in each batch.* Transfer lamb to large bowl using slotted spoon. Let cool to room temperature.

Add onion, kiwi, cilantro, chilies, capers, cashews, parsley, water chestnuts, mint, watercress, sesame seeds, lemon juice and salt and pepper to lamb and blend well. Arrange on large platter and garnish with reserved kiwi slices. Serve at room temperature.

Roasted Pepper Salad

12 servings

3 green bell peppers
2 red bell peppers

1 6-ounce jar marinated artichoke hearts, drained (reserve marinade) and patted dry
  Olive oil
8 ounces feta cheese, rinsed, patted dry and crumbled
2 6-ounce cans black olives, drained

³/₄ cup sliced mushrooms
¹/₂ cup sliced green onion
6 tablespoons minced fresh parsley
2 teaspoons minced garlic
1¹/₂ tablespoons dried oregano, crumbled
  Juice of 1¹/₂ lemons
  Salt and freshly ground pepper

  Toasted sesame seeds or additional feta cheese (garnish)

Preheat oven to 450°F. Place peppers on baking sheet and roast until skins are black and peppers are soft, about 30 minutes. Let cool slightly. Peel off skin. Cut peppers in half and discard stem and seeds; slice peppers thinly. Transfer to large serving bowl (preferably glass).

Combine reserved artichoke marinade in measuring cup with enough olive oil to equal 1¹/₃ cups. Pour over peppers. Add all remaining ingredients except garnish and toss well. Refrigerate at least 24 hours. (*Can be prepared up to 1 week ahead to this point and refrigerated.*)

Garnish with sesame seeds or feta. Serve salad at room temperature.

Peach Bombe with Boysenberry Sauce

12 servings

Bombe

1 quart rich French vanilla ice cream, softened
6 large peaches, peeled and pureed (about 1¹/₂ cups)
4 ounces shaved bittersweet chocolate
2 cups toasted chopped almonds
²/₃ cup Triple Sec or Grand Marnier
¹/₂ cup whipping cream
¹/₃ cup brandy

Boysenberry Sauce

3 cups (24 ounces) fresh or unsweetened frozen boysenberries, pureed and strained
¹/₂ cup sugar
¹/₂ cup softly whipped cream or crème fraîche (optional)
¹/₂ cup Triple Sec or Grand Marnier
¹/₄ cup brandy

For bombe: Oil 2-quart mold. Combine all ingredients in large bowl, blending well. Pour mixture into prepared mold and freeze until firm.

For sauce: Combine boysenberry puree, sugar, cream, liqueur and brandy in medium bowl, mixing well. Let stand at room temperature at least 1 hour.

To serve, run sharp thin knife around mold, dip bottom of mold quickly into hot water and invert onto platter. Serve with boysenberry sauce.

*Sweetened berries may be substituted; reduce or omit sugar.

Butterballs

Makes about 3 dozen

½ cup (1 stick) butter, room temperature
¼ cup sugar
2 tablespoons honey
1 cup plus 2 tablespoons all purpose flour

¼ teaspoon (scant) baking soda
2 tablespoons dark rum
1¼ cups coarsely ground walnuts or Brazil nuts

Powdered sugar

Cream butter, sugar and honey with electric mixer until smooth. Stir in flour and baking soda. Blend in rum, then nuts. Wrap dough in plastic and refrigerate until firm enough to handle, at least 1 hour, or overnight.

Preheat oven to 325°F. Lightly grease and flour baking sheets. Roll dough into 1-inch balls. Arrange on prepared sheets, spacing 1½ inches apart. Bake until firm and just beginning to color, 15 to 20 minutes. Cool slightly on racks. Roll in powdered sugar while still warm. Cool completely on racks. Store in airtight container.

 # *Light Picnic Lunch*

White Sangría
Three-Melon Soup of Summertime
Herbed Egg Salad Sandwich with
   Sliced Cucumbers and Westphalian Ham
Apple Candy Squares

Serves 4 to 6

White Sangría

About 6 servings

1 bottle (750 ml) dry white wine
½ cup orange liqueur
¼ cup sugar
1 orange, thinly sliced
1 lemon, thinly sliced

1 lime, thinly sliced
4 to 5 large strawberries, sliced
1 10-ounce bottle club soda
Ice cubes

Combine wine, liqueur and sugar in pitcher and stir until sugar is dissolved. Add sliced fruits. Cover and chill in refrigerator at least 1 hour to blend flavors. Just before serving add soda and ice cubes and stir gently to mix. Serve in wine glasses or Champagne flutes.

Three-Melon Soup of Summertime

6 servings

2 cups fresh orange juice
1½ cups finely chopped peeled cantaloupe
1½ cups finely chopped peeled Crenshaw melon
⅓ cup fresh lime juice
¼ cup honey
2 tablespoons sugar

2 tablespoons minced fresh mint or 1 teaspoon dried, crumbled
2 cups Asti Spumante or other sparkling white wine
1 cup finely chopped seeded watermelon
Fresh mint sprigs

Puree orange juice, cantaloupe, Crenshaw melon and lime juice in processor (in batches if necessary). Mix in honey, sugar and chopped mint. Pour puree into nonmetal container. Add wine and watermelon. Cover and refrigerate several hours or overnight. Garnish each serving with mint sprigs.

Herbed Egg Salad Sandwich with Sliced Cucumbers and Westphalian Ham

4 servings

¾ cup Homemade Mayonnaise*
¼ cup fresh parsley leaves
2 teaspoons chopped fresh dill or 1 teaspoon dried dillweed
1 medium-size green onion
Salt and freshly ground pepper
6 hard-cooked eggs, cooled and coarsely chopped
1 small celery stalk, peeled and chopped

1 1-pound loaf French bread
½ large cucumber, peeled, halved lengthwise, seeded and sliced (pat dry with paper towels)
8 thin slices smoked ham (preferably Westphalian)
Lettuce leaves

Combine ½ cup mayonnaise in processor work bowl with parsley, dill, onion, salt and pepper and mix well. Transfer to mixing bowl. Add eggs and celery and blend well. Adjust seasoning.

To assemble: Split bread lengthwise, but do not cut through. Open carefully and hollow out loaf, leaving ½-inch shell in each half. Spread remaining mayonnaise over each half. Arrange cucumber slices over bottom half of loaf. Spread egg salad over cucumbers. Layer ham slices over egg and top with lettuce. Close sandwich and press together gently. Secure with 6-inch wooden skewers. To serve, cut into 4 wedges.

*Homemade Mayonnaise

Makes 1¾ cups

1 egg
1 teaspoon fresh lemon juice
1 teaspoon red wine vinegar
1 teaspoon Dijon mustard
1 teaspoon salt

Freshly ground white pepper
1½ cups oil (preferably combination
of safflower and 3 tablespoons
olive oil)

Combine egg, lemon juice, vinegar, mustard, salt and pepper with 3 tablespoons oil in processor and mix until slightly thickened, about 8 seconds. With machine running, slowly add remaining oil through feed tube in thin, steady stream (once mayonnaise has thickened, oil can be added more quickly). Taste and adjust seasoning. Cover tightly and refrigerate.

Apple Candy Squares

Makes about 5 dozen

1¼ cups unsweetened applesauce
2 tablespoons unflavored gelatin
2 teaspoons fresh lemon juice
2 cups sugar

1 cup chopped walnuts
2 teaspoons vanilla
¾ to 1 cup powdered sugar

Line 8 × 8-inch baking pan with foil. Butter foil and set aside. Combine ½ cup applesauce, gelatin and lemon juice in small bowl and mix thoroughly. Let stand 10 minutes. Bring sugar and remaining ¾ cup applesauce to boil in heavy small saucepan. Whisk in gelatin mixture. Reduce heat to medium-low and return to boil, stirring constantly. Continue cooking until thick and glossy, about 15 minutes. Remove from heat. Stir in walnuts and vanilla. Turn into prepared pan, spreading evenly. Let stand uncovered at room temperature overnight. Cut into 1-inch squares. Roll in powdered sugar, coating completely. Store airtight.

Eclectic Grill Dinner

Rum Swizzle
Scallop Ceviche
Grilled ham steaks
Onion-Mustard Sauce
Endive-Cress Salad
Pecan Meringues

Serves 6

Rum Swizzle

6 servings

1 generous cup Jamaican rum
1 generous cup sweet vermouth

Angostura bitters
Freshly grated nutmeg

Pour rum and vermouth over ice in pitcher and mix well. Add about 6 dashes of bitters and grated nutmeg to taste. Serve immediately.

Scallop Ceviche

6 servings

1 pound bay scallops, rinsed, drained and patted dry
2 tablespoons fresh lemon juice
2 tablespoons raspberry vinegar
2 teaspoons olive oil
2 teaspoons safflower oil
½ teaspoon salt
Freshly ground pepper

½ small red onion, halved
1 large tomato, cored, seeded and coarsely chopped
3 tablespoons minced fresh basil
Basil leaves

Combine first 7 ingredients in plastic food storage bag. Seal bag and turn gently to mix. Refrigerate at least 8 hours, turning bag occasionally.

Drain scallops, discarding lemon juice mixture, and return to plastic bag.

Stand onion in processor feed tube and cut on French fry disc using firm pressure. Add to scallops with tomato. Seal bag and turn to mix. Chill 1 hour.

Just before serving, add minced basil to scallops. Divide among scallop shells or plates. Garnish with basil leaves.

Onion-Mustard Sauce

Serve over grilled ham steaks, or substitute this sauce for regular mustard on hamburgers or pork.

Makes 1 1/4 cups

1 cup chicken stock, preferably homemade
3/4 cup sliced onion
1/4 teaspoon minced garlic
1 cup whipping cream
1 1/2 tablespoons snipped fresh chives, sliced green onion or chopped fresh parsley

1 1/2 tablespoons coarse-grained mustard
1 tablespoon Dijon mustard
1 teaspoon fresh lemon juice
1/8 teaspoon freshly ground white pepper
Salt

Combine chicken stock, onion and garlic in heavy large skillet and bring to boil over medium-high heat. Continue boiling until reduced to slightly less than half. Whisk in cream and continue boiling until reduced to about 1 1/4 cups, skimming surface as necessary. (Sauce can be strained at this point if smoother texture is desired.) Stir in chives, mustards, lemon juice and pepper. Season with salt to taste. Serve immediately.

Endive-Cress Salad

6 servings

Dressing
3/4 cup walnut oil
6 tablespoons red wine vinegar
4 1/2 tablespoons minced shallot
3 tablespoons fresh lemon juice
Salt and freshly ground pepper

6 small Belgian endive, sliced crosswise 1/4 inch thick
3 small bunches watercress, tender top part only
3/4 cup chopped toasted walnuts

For dressing: Combine all ingredients for dressing in jar with tight-fitting lid and shake well. (*Can be prepared ahead.*)

Combine endive, watercress and walnuts and toss lightly. Cover and chill. Just before serving, add dressing to taste and toss gently but thoroughly.

Pecan Meringues

Serve these on their own or as an accompaniment to fruit, sherbet or ice cream.

Makes about 5 cups

3 jumbo egg whites, room temperature
1/2 teaspoon fresh lemon juice
Pinch of salt

2/3 cup sugar
3/4 teaspoon vanilla
3 cups pecan halves

Preheat oven to 175°F. Butter and flour nonstick baking sheets or line baking sheets with parchment. Beat whites with lemon juice and salt until soft peaks form. Add sugar 1 tablespoon at a time and beat until stiff and shiny. Add vanilla. Measure 3 cups meringue (discard any remaining) and fold in pecans. Spoon individual meringue-coated nuts on prepared sheets. Bake until beige and firm, about 2 1/4 hours. Cool completely before serving. Store in airtight container.

Holiday Reunion Barbecue

Watermelon Punch
Zucchini, Broccoli and Mushroom Salad
Grilled steak, hamburgers and hot dogs
Barbecued Potatoes in Foil
Ragout of Dried Fruits
Sweet Cornmeal Biscuits

Serves 10 to 12

Watermelon Punch

Makes about 2½ quarts

1 14-pound watermelon

2 pints strawberries, hulled
½ cup sugar
1 12-ounce can frozen lemonade
   concentrate, thawed

2 cups vodka (optional)

Fresh mint leaves

Sketch basket design on watermelon. (If necessary, cut slice from bottom so melon stands upright.) Carve melon using long thin knife. Remove melon pulp with ice cream scoop.

Process pulp in processor in batches until smooth. Strain through sieve into large bowl until juice measures 7 cups (reserve any remaining pulp for another use). Blend 1½ pints of strawberries with sugar until smooth, about 10 seconds. Stir into watermelon juice with lemonade concentrate and vodka. Chill.

Just before serving, fill melon cavity with some of punch. Slice remaining ½ pint of strawberries; float atop punch. Garnish with mint leaves. Refill basket with punch as necessary.

Zucchini, Broccoli and Mushroom Salad

12 servings

2 bunches broccoli, broken into
   bite-size florets, stems peeled and
   cut diagonally into bite-size
   pieces

8 small zucchini, thinly sliced
1 cup water
½ cup red wine vinegar
2 teaspoons dried savory, crumbled

¾ cup olive oil
½ cup capers, rinsed and drained

⅓ cup chopped pimiento
3 green onions, thinly sliced
1 teaspoon Dijon mustard
   Salt and freshly ground pepper
8 ounces mushrooms

Boston lettuce leaves

Drop broccoli into large quantity of boiling salted water and cook until crisp-tender, about 4 to 5 minutes. Drain well and chill.

Cook zucchini in 1 cup water with ¼ cup wine vinegar and savory until crisp-tender, about 3 minutes. Drain well; cover and refrigerate.

Combine olive oil, remaining ¼ cup vinegar, capers, pimiento, onion, mustard, salt and pepper in jar with tight-fitting lid and shake well. Thinly slice mushrooms into bowl; pour dressing over and mix thoroughly.

Line salad bowl with lettuce. Add broccoli, zucchini and mushrooms with dressing and toss lightly. Serve immediately.

Barbecued Potatoes in Foil

10 to 12 servings

Corn oil
5 pounds potatoes, peeled and thinly sliced
3 yellow onions, thinly sliced

½ cup (1 stick) butter, cut into small pieces
Salt and freshly ground pepper

Fold two 24-inch-long sheets of heavy-duty foil in half. Place one sheet crosswise over the other. Coat generously with oil. Combine potatoes and onion in center of foil. Mix in butter and season with salt and pepper. Wrap foil tightly, forming large bag.

Prepare barbecue. When gray ash has formed, lay foil bag directly on coals. Cook, turning about every 10 minutes, for about 1 hour.

To serve, slit bag in center. Use large spoon to loosen potato slices clinging to foil. Make sure each serving contains some of these crusty brown slices as well as potatoes from center.

Ragout of Dried Fruits

Any combination of dried fruits can be used in this tasty compote.

12 servings

2 pounds dried fruits (such as apricots, peaches, pears, prunes, cherries)
2 750-ml bottles Moscato or other dessert wine
6 tablespoons honey

¼ cup plus 2 teaspoons fresh lemon juice
Generous pinch of salt
Julienne of lemon peel (optional)

Combine fruits, wine and honey in heavy large nonaluminum saucepan. Bring to boil. Reduce heat and simmer until fruit is tender, stirring occasionally, about 15 minutes. Cool. Mix in lemon juice and salt. Refrigerate at least 2 hours. (*Can be prepared 1 day ahead.*) Let stand at room temperature 20 minutes before serving. Garnish with lemon peel.

Sweet Cornmeal Biscuits

Makes about 4½ dozen

10 tablespoons (1¼ sticks) unsalted butter, room temperature
3 ounces chilled cream cheese
¾ cup sugar
1 egg
1 teaspoon vanilla

½ generous teaspoon freshly ground pepper
Pinch of salt
1 cup cornmeal
1¾ cups unbleached all purpose flour, sifted

Using electric mixer, cream butter and cream cheese until fluffy. Gradually add sugar, beating until fluffy. Mix in egg, vanilla, pepper and salt. Beat in cornmeal. Fold in flour using rubber spatula. Form dough into two 2-inch-diameter cylinders. Wrap each in foil and refrigerate overnight.

Preheat oven to 350°F. Grease baking sheets. Cut cookie dough into ⅜-inch-thick slices. Arrange on prepared sheets, spacing ½ inch apart. Bake until edges are golden brown, 17 to 19 minutes. Cool on racks.

 # Cool Summertime Brunch

Mr. G's Famous Ramos Fizz
Smoked Salmon and Caper Whip with
   Sliced Tomatoes and Onions
Salad of Mushrooms and Watercress
Special Toffee Bars

Serves 6

Mr. G's Famous Ramos Fizz

Best prepared in two-serving batches.

2 servings

3 ounces (6 tablespoons) gin
2 tablespoons plus 1 teaspoon fresh lemon juice
1 generous tablespoon sugar
¾ cup half and half

1 egg white
12 drops orange flower water
8 ice cubes
Freshly grated nutmeg

Mix first 3 ingredients in blender on high speed 15 seconds. Add half and half, egg white, orange flower water and 4 ice cubes and blend 30 seconds. Divide remaining ice cubes between 2 brandy snifters. Pour gin mixture over ice. Sprinkle with nutmeg and serve immediately.

Smoked Salmon and Caper Whip with Sliced Tomatoes and Onions

*For six servings, prepare
two sandwiches to allow
for hearty appetites.*

4 servings

8 ounces cream cheese
(room temperature), halved
¼ cup fresh parsley leaves
2 tablespoons fresh lemon juice
1 tablespoon milk, sour cream or
whipping cream
1 teaspoon capers, rinsed and
drained
4 ounces smoked Nova Scotia
salmon

1 1-pound loaf French bread
1 medium tomato, cored and sliced
1 very small onion (1 ounce), sliced

Combine cream cheese, parsley, lemon juice, milk and capers with 3 ounces
salmon in processor and mix until smooth, stopping machine once to scrape
down sides of work bowl. Add remaining salmon and mix briefly until just
incorporated (retain texture of salmon as much as possible).

To assemble: Split bread lengthwise, but do not cut through. Open carefully
and hollow out loaf, leaving ½-inch shell in each half. Divide salmon mixture
and spread evenly over both halves. Layer tomato slices over bottom half of loaf.
Top with onion. Close sandwich and press together gently. Secure with 6-inch
wooden skewers. To serve, cut diagonally into 4 wedges.

Salad of Mushrooms and Watercress

6 servings

¼ cup balsamic vinegar
½ teaspoon salt
½ teaspoon (scant) Dijon mustard
¾ cup olive oil

12 ounces mushrooms, quartered

1½ cups watercress leaves

Mix vinegar, salt and mustard in large bowl. Gradually whisk in oil in thin stream.
Stir in mushrooms. Let marinate 30 minutes, stirring occasionally.

Just before serving, add watercress to salad and toss to coat with dressing.

Special Toffee Bars

Makes about 3 dozen

1 cup (2 sticks) butter or
margarine, room temperature
1 cup firmly packed light
brown sugar
1 egg yolk
1 teaspoon vanilla
2 cups all purpose flour

¼ teaspoon salt
4 1.45-ounce milk chocolate bars,
separated into pieces
½ cup finely chopped almonds,
walnuts or pecans

Preheat oven to 350°F. Grease 9 × 13-inch baking pan. Beat butter, brown sugar,
yolk and vanilla in large bowl until smooth. Stir in flour and salt and blend well.
Pat evenly into bottom of prepared pan. Bake until golden, about 25 minutes.
Place chocolate evenly over top and let stand until softened, about 5 minutes;
spread thinly. Sprinkle nuts over chocolate. Cut into 1½-inch bars while still
warm. Store in airtight container.

Middle Eastern Kebab Grill

Middle Eastern Chickpea Soup
Barbecued Beef Kebabs in Onion Marinade
Egyptian Salad
Coconut Rice Pudding

Serves 4 to 6

Middle Eastern Chickpea Soup

Served hot or cold, this is the ideal starter for a meal of seafood, meat kebabs or roast lamb. Accompany with buttered and toasted pita bread.

4 servings

3 tablespoons olive oil
1 15-ounce can chickpeas (garbanzo beans), rinsed and drained
2 large onions, chopped
2 large garlic cloves, chopped
3 bay leaves
1 teaspoon grated lemon peel
½ teaspoon whole cumin seeds, ground
¼ teaspoon whole coriander seeds, ground

⅛ teaspoon turmeric
3 cups rich meat or poultry stock

Salt and freshly ground pepper
2 to 4 tablespoons fresh lemon juice
¼ cup Italian parsley, minced
¼ cup fresh mint leaves, minced
1 large garlic clove, minced

Heat oil in heavy 2½- to 3-quart saucepan over low heat. Mix in chickpeas, onions, garlic, bay leaves, lemon peel, cumin and coriander. Cover and cook until onions are soft, stirring occasionally, about 10 minutes. Mix in turmeric. Cover and cook 10 minutes, stirring occasionally. Add stock. Cover partially and simmer 10 minutes. Cool.

Discard bay leaf. Transfer ¾ cup chickpea and onion mixture to bowl using slotted spoon. Puree remaining soup in blender until smooth. Add reserved chickpeas and onions and chop coarsely. (*Can be prepared 2 days ahead, covered and refrigerated.*)

Reheat soup. Season with salt and generous amount of pepper. Add lemon juice to taste. Ladle soup into heated bowls. Combine parsley, mint and garlic. Swirl into soup to taste.

For variation, refrigerate soup to chill. Whisk in 1 cup plain yogurt, adding water to thin if desired. Swirl parsley-mint mixture into soup just before serving.

Barbecued Beef Kebabs in Onion Marinade

4 servings

½ large onion, grated
¼ teaspoon ground cumin
¼ teaspoon fresh lemon juice
¼ teaspoon cider vinegar
⅛ teaspoon garlic powder
  Crushed red pepper flakes
  (optional)
1 pound top sirloin, cut into
  12 cubes
  Salt and freshly ground pepper

8 cherry tomatoes (optional)
1 green bell pepper, cored, seeded
  and cubed
1 large onion, cubed

Combine onion, cumin, lemon juice, vinegar, garlic powder and red pepper flakes in small bowl. Season beef generously with salt and pepper. Rub cumin mixture into beef. Set aside 30 minutes.

Prepare barbecue grill. Alternate meat, tomatoes, green pepper and onion on 4 skewers. Barbecue to desired doneness and serve.

Egyptian Salad

4 to 6 servings

½ head romaine lettuce, torn into
  ½-inch strips
2 large tomatoes, cut into
  bite-size pieces
1 green bell pepper, cored, seeded
  and cut into ½-inch cubes
½ yellow onion, cut into
  1-inch strips
½ cucumber, quartered and
  chopped into ½-inch pieces

2 to 3 tablespoons chopped
  fresh parsley
1 tablespoon fresh lime juice
½ teaspoon cider vinegar
½ teaspoon salt
¼ teaspoon ground cumin
¼ teaspoon garlic powder
⅛ teaspoon crushed red pepper
  flakes (optional)

Combine lettuce, tomatoes, green pepper, onion, cucumber and parsley in large bowl. Just before serving, sprinkle remaining ingredients over top of salad and toss thoroughly.

Coconut Rice Pudding

The rose water gives this pudding an exotic nuance.

6 servings

2½ cups water
1 cup long-grain white rice
2 cups milk, room temperature
½ cup shredded coconut
⅔ cup sugar

1 teaspoon rose water
½ teaspoon vanilla
  Cinnamon
  Chopped unsalted pistachios

Bring water to boil in medium saucepan. Stir in rice. Reduce heat to low, cover and cook 10 minutes. Add milk and coconut. Increase heat to medium and cook, stirring constantly, 20 minutes. Blend in sugar. Remove from heat. Mix in rose water and vanilla. Divide pudding evenly among dessert cups or bowls. Sprinkle with cinnamon and nuts. Chill until ready to serve.

🍒 *All-American Rib Barbecue*

Bourbon Fruit Cooler
Spareribs with Alabama Barbecue Sauce
Elko Basque Festival Beans
Buttermilk Biscuits
Coca-Cola Cake

Serves 6

Bourbon Fruit Cooler

Makes 6 cups

1 6-ounce can frozen pineapple juice concentrate (unthawed)
2 medium bananas (6 ounces each), peeled and cut into several pieces
1 cup ice cubes
2 tablespoons sugar
1½ cups club soda
⅔ cup bourbon

Combine pineapple juice concentrate, banana, ice cubes and sugar in processor and mix using 6 on/off turns, then blend until smooth. Transfer to chilled pitcher. Stir in soda and bourbon. Serve immediately.

Spareribs with Alabama Barbecue Sauce

Home-style ribs with a sweet-spicy basting sauce. Refrigerated sauce will keep up to two weeks.

6 servings

Alabama Barbecue Sauce
2 tablespoons vegetable oil
1 onion, minced
1 large garlic clove, minced
½ cup catsup
½ cup cider vinegar
⅓ cup honey
¼ cup Worcestershire sauce

Juice of 1 lemon
2 teaspoons dry mustard
1 teaspoon ground ginger
1 teaspoon salt

4 pounds pork spareribs, well trimmed

Heat oil in medium saucepan over low heat. Add onion and garlic and sauté until soft. Add all remaining ingredients (except ribs) and simmer 15 minutes. Remove from heat and set aside.

Heat coals until gray ash forms. Spread into overlapping layer and let burn 20 minutes. Set grill about 3 inches above coals. (Fire should be gentle so ribs do not burn. If it seems too hot, spread coals further apart; if too slow, add more coals and push together.)

Arrange ribs on grill and cook slowly 30 minutes, turning once. Brush ribs generously with sauce and cook another 20 minutes. Turn ribs, brush again with sauce and cook 20 minutes longer. Serve hot.

Elko Basque Festival Beans

The biggest and best known of Nevada's numerous Basque festivals, Elko's is held every July.

Makes 6 quarts

3 pounds dried pinto beans
3 slices bacon, chopped
1 large onion, chopped
1 10-ounce can tomatoes, undrained
1 8-ounce piece lean ham or small ham hock
2 chorizo sausages (8 ounces total), sliced
1 tablespoon (about) salt

Discard any discolored beans. Rinse remainder under cold running water. Drain well. Transfer to large bowl. Add enough cold water to cover. Let soak at least 8 hours or overnight.

Fry bacon in large skillet over medium heat just until crisp. Add chopped onion and sauté until golden, about 3 to 4 minutes. Stir in tomatoes. Reduce heat to low and simmer 20 minutes. Drain beans; transfer to stockpot or Dutch oven. Add tomato mixture, ham and sausage. Add enough cold water to cover. Bring to boil over high heat. Reduce heat to low, cover partially and simmer 2 hours, stirring occasionally. Add salt and continue to cook 1 hour, stirring occasionally. Serve hot.

Basque Festival Beans can be prepared ahead. Cool to room temperature, cover and refrigerate. Reheat before serving.

Buttermilk Biscuits

These large, soft biscuits are a natural with butter and honey. Serve straight from the oven with the barbecued ribs.

Makes 6

2 cups sifted unbleached all purpose flour
2 teaspoons baking powder
¼ teaspoon baking soda
¼ teaspoon salt
6 tablespoons solid vegetable shortening, room temperature
1 cup buttermilk

Position rack in center of oven and preheat to 450°F. Sift flour, baking powder, baking soda and salt into medium bowl. Cut in shortening until mixture resembles coarse meal. Make well in center. Add buttermilk to well. Stir just until mixture is moistened.

Generously flour hands. Divide dough into 6 pieces. Lightly toss each piece back and forth between hands to form ball. Arrange on ungreased baking sheet. Flatten to 1-inch rounds; sides should touch. Bake until light brown, 18 to 20 minutes. Cool biscuits for 5 minutes on rack before serving.

Coca-Cola Cake

A very sweet dessert that is extremely popular in the South—especially in Vicksburg, Mississippi, the first city to bottle this soft drink.

Makes one 9 × 13-inch cake

Cake
2 cups all purpose flour
2 cups sugar
1 cup (2 sticks) butter
1 cup Coca-Cola
2 tablespoons unsweetened cocoa powder
½ cup buttermilk
2 eggs
2 teaspoons vanilla
1 teaspoon baking soda
¼ teaspoon salt
1½ cups miniature marshmallows

Icing
½ cup (1 stick) butter
6 tablespoons Coca-Cola
2 tablespoons unsweetened cocoa powder
1 pound powdered sugar
1 teaspoon vanilla
1 cup chopped pecans

For cake: Preheat oven to 350°F. Butter 9 × 13-inch baking pan. Sift flour and sugar into large bowl. Melt 1 cup butter in heavy small saucepan. Add Coca-Cola and cocoa powder and bring just to boil. Stir into flour mixture. Blend in buttermilk, eggs, vanilla, baking soda and salt. Fold in marshmallows. Pour into pan. Bake until tester inserted in center comes out clean, about 35 minutes.

Meanwhile, prepare icing: Melt butter in heavy medium saucepan. Add Coca-Cola and cocoa powder and bring just to boil. Remove from heat. Stir in powdered sugar and vanilla. Fold in pecans. Spread icing over hot cake. Serve warm or at room temperature.

Southeast Asian Skewer Grill

Scallop Kebabs
Vietnamese Pork Sticks with Lettuce Cups
Cucumber Stick Salad
Gingered Fruit Salad

Serves 4

Scallop Kebabs

8 appetizer or 3 to 4 main-course servings

12 strips thinly sliced bacon, partially cooked until light brown and cut into pieces same size as scallops	2 tablespoons rice vinegar
16 sea scallops, halved horizontally	1½ tablespoons sugar
16 small water chestnuts, halved horizontally	1 tablespoon Chinese rice wine or dry Sherry
32 5- to 6-inch bamboo skewers	1 garlic clove, minced
⅓ cup soy sauce	1 teaspoon minced fresh ginger

Alternate bacon between scallop and water chestnut slices on skewers. Arrange in shallow dish. Combine remaining ingredients in processor or blender and mix well. Pour over kebabs, cover and marinate in refrigerator for 2 to 3 hours, turning frequently.

Prepare fire, allowing coals to burn down to moderate temperature. Set grill about 4 inches above coals.

Spread coals in single layer. Drain off marinade and pat kebabs dry with paper towels. Grill until scallops are barely firm, about 6 minutes per side, and serve immediately.

Vietnamese Pork Sticks with Lettuce Cups

Tempting finger food with a delicious sauce.

4 servings

Meat Mixture
- 1 pound finely ground lean pork butt
- 6 water chestnuts, minced
- 1 large garlic clove, minced
- 1 small green onion, minced
- 1 tablespoon Japanese soy sauce
- 2 teaspoons vegetable oil
- 1¼ teaspoons fresh lemon juice
- ½ teaspoon minced fresh ginger
- ¼ teaspoon sugar
- ¼ teaspoon Chinese hot chili oil
- ⅛ teaspoon salt

- 12 5- to 6-inch bamboo skewers

Garnishes
- 12 Boston or Bibb lettuce leaves
- ½ cup chopped cilantro
- ½ cup chopped fresh mint leaves
- ½ cup chopped green onion

Dipping Sauce
- ½ cup Japanese soy sauce
- 5 tablespoons fresh lemon juice
- 3 tablespoons water
- 2 garlic cloves, minced
- 2 teaspoons sugar
- 1 teaspoon oyster sauce
- 1 teaspoon minced fresh ginger
- ⅛ to ¼ teaspoon cayenne pepper

For meat: Combine all ingredients in large bowl and use hands to mix gently but thoroughly. Shape into 12 cylinders approximately 3 inches long and no more than 1 inch thick. Insert bamboo skewer through each cylinder.

For garnishes: Arrange garnishes in separate bowls; refrigerate.

For sauce: Combine all ingredients in small saucepan and bring to boil. Reduce heat and simmer 5 minutes. Let cool. Divide among 4 small bowls.

Heat coals until gray ash forms. Spread into overlapping layer, knocking off ash so coals are hot and glowing. Place grill 2 to 3 inches above coals.

Arrange pork sticks on grill so they do not touch. Cook until meat is crisped, browned and firm, turning often with tongs, about 10 to 15 minutes.

Have each diner sprinkle lettuce leaf with other garnishes. Slip pork off skewer onto lettuce. Wrap around pork and use sauce for dipping.

Meat mixture can be prepared and skewered up to 24 hours before barbecuing. Sauce will keep 2 weeks in refrigerator.

Cucumber Stick Salad

4 servings

- 2 cucumbers, peeled, halved horizontally, seeded and cut into thin sticks
- 1 tablespoon cider vinegar or rice vinegar or to taste

- 2 teaspoons soy sauce
- 1 teaspoon sugar or to taste
  Few dashes oriental sesame oil

Place cucumbers in mixing bowl. Cover and refrigerate overnight. Drain off accumulated liquid. Add remaining ingredients and toss well. Serve chilled.

Gingered Fruit Salad

Makes about 5 cups

⅔ cup fresh orange juice
1½ tablespoons fresh lemon juice
1 tablespoon honey
1 tablespoon ginger-flavored brandy or brandy
2 large bananas, sliced
2 large cooking apples, cored and chopped

10 dried apricot halves, finely chopped
2 teaspoons finely chopped crystallized ginger

1 kiwi fruit, peeled and sliced

Combine juices, honey and brandy in small bowl. Mix bananas, apples, dried apricots and ginger in large bowl. Pour brandy sauce over and toss well. Cover and refrigerate at least 1 hour or overnight.
   Spoon salad into bowls. Garnish with kiwi and serve.

 # Stylish Barbecue on the Deck

Iced Puree of Vegetables and Herbs
Herb-scented Tenderloin with Mustard Caper Sauce
Grilled Green Onions
Gruyère-stuffed Potatoes with Sour Cream
Apricot Squares

Serves 6 to 8

Iced Puree of Vegetables and Herbs

8 servings

2 tablespoons (¼ stick) butter
1 pound leeks, cut into 1-inch slices
½ cup coarsely chopped celery (including leaves)
3 tablespoons fresh lemon juice

1 cup shelled fresh green peas
1 cup finely shredded fresh spinach or Swiss chard

1 cup finely shredded lettuce
5 cups chicken stock
2 cups half and half
   Salt and freshly ground pepper
1 tablespoon minced fresh parsley
1 tablespoon minced fresh mint leaves or 1 teaspoon dried, crumbled

Melt butter in heavy large saucepan over low heat. Add leeks, celery and lemon juice and cook until leeks are tender, about 15 minutes, stirring mixture occasionally.
   Stir in peas, spinach and lettuce. Add stock, increase heat and bring to boil. Reduce heat and simmer until all vegetables are tender, about 10 minutes. Blend in half and half. Puree soup in batches in blender. Strain soup through fine sieve. Season with salt and pepper to taste. Refrigerate several hours or overnight. Stir in parsley and mint just before serving.

Herb-scented Tenderloin with Mustard Caper Sauce

Served at "patio" temperature, this rosy-rare simple-to-do beef dish is the star of the summer buffet table.

6 to 8 servings

1 4-pound beef tenderloin butt, trimmed of all fat
3 tablespoons olive oil
8 branches fresh marjoram or

oregano (or 4 tablespoons crumbled dried leaves)

Mustard Caper Sauce*

Let tenderloin stand at room temperature 30 minutes. Rub all sides with oil.

Heat coals until gray ash forms. Spread into overlapping layer and let burn 15 minutes. Set grill 3 inches above coals.

Set beef on grill and cook about 8 minutes. Turn and continue cooking, frequently sprinkling coals with herbs, until meat thermometer inserted in thickest part of meat registers 125°F (very rare), 130°F (rare) or 135°F (medium-rare). Remove and let cool.

When ready to serve, slice meat thinly and arrange on platter in overlapping pattern. Spoon ribbon of sauce down center; pass remainder.

*Mustard Caper Sauce

Makes about 1½ cups

3 generous tablespoons coarse-grained mustard
2 egg yolks, room temperature
1 small green onion, chopped
¼ teaspoon chopped fresh marjoram or pinch of dried, crumbled

Juice of ½ large lemon (about 2 tablespoons)
1 cup light olive oil, room temperature
¼ to ½ cup whipping cream
1½ tablespoons capers, rinsed and drained

Combine first 5 ingredients in processor and mix until pale and creamy. With machine running, gradually add oil through feed tube in thin stream, stopping machine occasionally to be sure oil is absorbed. Add cream and capers and mix until thoroughly blended.

Sauce can be prepared up to 3 days ahead and refrigerated. Serve at room temperature.

Grilled Green Onions

Grill the onions while the fire is still hot, then cool to room temperature while cooking the tenderloin. Good with any other grilled meat, poultry or fish, too.

8 servings

32 large green onions, trimmed, with 2 inches of green tops
1 cup olive oil

1 large garlic clove, minced
⅛ teaspoon freshly ground pepper
Salt

Combine all ingredients in shallow pan. Marinate at least 3 hours. (*Can be prepared 1 day ahead and refrigerated.*)

Prepare barbecue with hot coals. Drain green onions. Grill on all sides until light brown. Transfer to platter. Serve onions at room temperature.

Gruyère-stuffed Potatoes with Sour Cream

6 servings

6 medium baking potatoes
(3 pounds total)
¾ teaspoon vegetable oil

1 cup sour cream
1 teaspoon salt
Freshly ground pepper
Freshly grated nutmeg

3½ ounces Gruyère cheese,
room temperature, cut into
1-inch pieces

2 tablespoons snipped fresh chives

Position rack in center of oven and preheat to 425°F. Scrub potatoes and pat dry. Brush with oil. Bake until tender, about 1 hour. Seal in paper bag and let stand 15 minutes.

Cut ¾-inch-thick horizontal slice from top of each potato. Scoop pulp from potatoes into bowl, reserving shells. Mash pulp using ricer, masher or mixer. Add sour cream, salt, pepper and nutmeg and mix until fluffy.

Finely mince cheese in processor. Fold into potato mixture. Spoon into potato shells, mounding slightly. (*Can be prepared 1 day ahead and chilled. Bring to room temperature before continuing.*)

Prepare barbecue. Place potatoes on grill. Cover barbecue and cook until potatoes are heated and puffed, about 25 minutes. Sprinkle with snipped chives and serve immediately.

Apricot Squares

Makes 35 1½-inch squares

1 cup (2 sticks) butter,
room temperature
1 cup sugar
1 egg yolk

2 cups all purpose flour
¾ cup finely chopped walnuts

1 10-ounce jar apricot jam

Preheat oven to 350°F. Cream butter with sugar in large bowl. Add egg yolk and mix well. Stir in flour. Add walnuts and blend well (dough will be soft).

Divide dough in half. Spread half evenly into bottom of 9 × 13-inch baking dish. Cover with apricot jam. Drop remaining dough by spoonfuls over jam, spreading carefully to edges with knife. Bake until top is golden, about 40 to 45 minutes. Let cool slightly before cutting into squares.

James Scherer

*Clockwise from right:
Summer Garden Salad;
Grilled Swordfish with
Mustard Sauce; Tomato
Filled with Corn Pudding;
Portuguese Sweet Bread*

Left to right:
Tomato-Yogurt Soup; Cold
Mint-Cucumber Soup;
Cold Melon Soup

*Left to right: Herbed Prosciutto
Flatbread; Veal and Chicken Loaf
with Arugula Sauce; Carrot and
Red Pepper Slaw*

Creamy Carrot Soup

Clockwise from left:
Sausage and White Bean Pâté with Tomato Sauce; Gorgonzola with Madeira; Marinated Lamb Salad

Brian Leatart

Strawberries on the Half Shell

Picnic with a Handsome Hero

Vegetable Hero Sandwich
Mustard Potato Salad
Coconut Chocolate Bars

Serves 4 to 6

Vegetable Hero Sandwich

Secure this sandwich with six-inch wooden skewers to facilitate slicing and to maintain the layering.

4 to 6 servings

Filling
- ¹/₂ medium-size green bell pepper
- 2 ounces green beans, trimmed and cut into 1¹/₂-inch lengths
- 1 small red onion (2 ounces)
- 4 large radishes, trimmed
- 4 medium cauliflower florets
- 1 4-ounce piece hard salami or smoked sausage
- 2 Italian plum tomatoes

- 4 ounces chilled Monterey Jack cheese
- 1 2-ounce piece carrot

- 2 small dill pickles (1 ounce total)
- 2 canned hot Italian peppers (optional)

- 1 1-pound loaf French bread
  Softened butter
  Bavarian-style mustard
  Mayonnaise, preferably homemade
  Swiss chard leaves, spinach leaves or leaf lettuce
- 1 cup (16 tablespoons) Italian Dressing*

For filling: In processor, slice or shred each ingredient separately as follows, transferring to work surface in individual groups.

Thin or medium slicer: Slice green pepper, green beans and red onion using medium pressure. Slice radishes, cauliflower and salami using firm pressure. Slice tomatoes using light pressure.

Shredder: Shred cheese using light pressure. Shred carrot using firm pressure. Shred dill pickles and hot Italian peppers using light pressure.

To assemble: Split bread lengthwise, but do not cut through. Open carefully and hollow out loaf, leaving ¹/₂-inch shell in each half. Spread halves with butter, mustard and mayonnaise (in that order). Arrange greens in single layer over both sides. Distribute vegetables over greens as evenly as possible. Spoon 6 tablespoons Italian dressing over filling. Close sandwich and secure edges with 6-inch wooden skewers. To serve, cut sandwich into 4 to 6 pieces. Pass remaining dressing separately.

*Italian Dressing

Makes 1 cup

- ¹/₄ cup fresh parsley leaves
- 2 medium garlic cloves
- ³/₄ cup vegetable oil
- ¹/₄ cup red wine vinegar

- 1 teaspoon Bavarian-style mustard
- 1 teaspoon salt
  Freshly ground black pepper

Mince parsley in processor using on/off turns. Mince garlic by dropping through feed tube with machine running. Add remaining ingredients and blend well.

Mustard Potato Salad

4 to 6 servings

3 pounds boiling potatoes
3 teaspoons coarse kosher salt
3 eggs, room temperature

½ cup chopped green onion
5 tablespoons balsamic or red wine vinegar
3 tablespoons olive oil
1 thyme sprig, minced, or ¼ teaspoon dried, crumbled
Freshly ground pepper

2 celery stalks, trimmed and chopped
1 small hot red chili or jalapeño pepper, seeded and finely chopped

1½ cups (about) Classic Mayonnaise*
3 tablespoons plain yogurt
2 tablespoons plus 1 teaspoon fresh lemon juice
2 tablespoons Dijon mustard
⅓ cup minced fresh parsley or mixture of parsley and other fresh herbs
Tomato wedges
Minced fresh parsley
Thyme sprig (optional)

Place potatoes in large saucepan and cover with cold water. Cover saucepan and bring to boil. Add 2 teaspoons salt and eggs. Cover partially and boil 11 minutes. Remove eggs using slotted spoon. Rinse under cold water to cool. Continue cooking potatoes until tender. Drain potatoes in colander and rinse with cold water until just cool enough to handle.

Cut potatoes into 1-inch chunks. Combine with green onion, vinegar, oil, minced thyme, pepper and remaining 1 teaspoon salt in large bowl. Let cool.

Add celery and hot chili to potatoes. Combine 1 cup mayonnaise, yogurt, lemon juice and mustard in small bowl. Gently mix into salad. Adjust seasoning. Chop eggs coarsely. Add to salad with ⅓ cup parsley. Toss gently. (*Can be prepared 6 hours ahead and refrigerated. Let stand at room temperature 15 minutes before continuing.*) Just before serving, mix in as much of remaining mayonnaise as desired. Garnish with tomatoes, parsley and thyme sprig.

*Classic Mayonnaise

Makes about 2 cups

2 egg yolks, room temperature
3 tablespoons fresh lemon juice
½ teaspoon salt

Pinch of cayenne pepper
¾ cup olive oil
¾ cup vegetable oil

Blend yolks, lemon juice, salt and cayenne pepper in processor. With machine running, slowly pour both oils through feed tube in thin stream.

Coconut Chocolate Bars

Makes 16

3 eggs
1 cup sugar
½ cup (1 stick) margarine, room temperature
2 cups semisweet chocolate chips
1 cup pecan halves

1 cup flaked coconut
½ cup all purpose flour
2 tablespoons unsweetened cocoa powder
1 teaspoon vanilla

Preheat oven to 350°F. Butter 8-inch square baking pan. Using electric mixer, beat eggs until foamy, about 1 minute. Add sugar and beat until fluffy, about 1 minute. Beat in margarine until well blended, about 1 minute. Stir in 1 cup chocolate chips, pecans, coconut, flour, cocoa powder and vanilla. Pour into prepared pan. Bake until just set but still very moist and sticky, about 20 minutes. Scatter remaining chocolate chips over and let stand until softened, 2 to 3 minutes. Spread chocolate over top. Cool slightly. Cut into bars and serve warm.

 # *Tuscan Dinner* alla Griglia

Champagne with Campari and Orange Slices
Chilled Tuscan Bean Soup
Charcoal-grilled steak with Anchovy Sauce
Salad of mixed greens and radicchio
Italian bread
Pears Poached in Red Wine
Hazelnut Pepper Cookies

Serves 6

Champagne with Campari and Orange Slices

6 servings

1 bottle chilled Champagne
6 tablespoons chilled Campari

1 tablespoon Cognac
½ firm seedless orange, sliced

Combine Champagne, Campari and Cognac in large pitcher and stir gently just until blended. Pour into glasses and garnish each with orange slice. Serve immediately.

Chilled Tuscan Bean Soup

6 servings

2 tablespoons olive oil
1 small onion, minced
1 garlic clove, minced
4 ounces cabbage, coarsely chopped (about 1½ firmly packed cups)
4 ounces zucchini, cut into ¼-inch-thick slices
2 medium leeks, thinly sliced
1 cup drained canned Italian plum tomatoes
1 medium carrot, finely chopped
1 small celery stalk, finely chopped

½ teaspoon minced fresh rosemary or ¼ teaspoon dried, crumbled
¼ teaspoon dried red pepper flakes
Salt
3 cups water
2 cups beef consommé (or more)
8 ounces small dried Great Northern beans

6 ½-inch-thick slices Italian bread
1 garlic clove, halved
3 tablespoons olive oil
Freshly grated Parmesan cheese

Heat 2 tablespoons olive oil in heavy large saucepan over medium-high heat. Add onion and garlic and sauté 2 to 3 minutes. Add cabbage, zucchini, leeks, tomatoes, carrot, celery, rosemary, red pepper flakes and salt and cook until vegetables begin to soften, about 6 minutes. Add water, 2 cups consommé and beans and bring to boil. Reduce heat, cover and simmer until beans are tender, about 1½ hours, stirring occasionally.

Puree soup in batches in blender. Chill several hours or up to 1 week.

To serve, thin soup with additional consommé if desired. Toast bread; rub lightly with cut sides of garlic clove. Brush bread with most of remaining oil. Ladle soup into individual bowls. Top with crouton and sprinkle with cheese. Place several drops of remaining oil into each bowl.

Anchovy Sauce

When chilled, this is perfect for melting over broiled steak. Served at room temperature it makes a savory complement to mild fish such as cod or flounder.

Makes 1 cup

8 anchovy fillets (or more to taste)
2 egg yolks, room temperature
1 small garlic clove
2 to 2½ tablespoons fresh lemon juice
½ cup (1 stick) butter, melted and hot

½ cup vegetable oil, heated
6 parsley sprigs, stemmed
¼ teaspoon freshly ground pepper

Combine anchovy fillets, egg yolks and garlic in processor and mix 30 seconds. Add 1 tablespoon lemon juice and blend well. Mix butter and oil together. With machine running, add ¼ cup butter mixture through feed tube 1 drop at a time, then add remaining ¾ cup butter mixture in slow steady stream; *do not stop machine at any point.* Add another tablespoon lemon juice with parsley and pepper and mix using on/off turns until parsley is chopped. Taste and season with remaining lemon juice if desired. If sauce is too thick, add small amount of warm water, blending well. Serve chilled or at room temperature.

Pears Poached in Red Wine

These pears marinate for two days before serving, so they can absorb flavor.

6 servings

2 cups dry red wine
½ cup sugar
2 tablespoons fresh lemon juice

1 2-inch cinnamon stick
6 small firm-ripe pears, peeled, halved and cored

Combine first 4 ingredients in large nonaluminum saucepan and bring to boil over medium-high heat, stirring until sugar dissolves. Add pears and partially cover pan. Simmer very gently over low heat until pears are soft but not mushy, about 15 to 20 minutes. Let cool, then transfer to bowl. Cover and refrigerate 2 days before serving, turning pears occasionally so they color evenly.

Hazelnut Pepper Cookies

Can be stored at room temperature for five days or frozen about four months.

Makes about 9 dozen cookies

3 ounces hazelnuts, shelled, toasted and skinned
1 cup all purpose flour
½ cup sugar
½ teaspoon freshly ground pepper
⅛ teaspoon salt
2 generous pinches whole aniseed, ground

½ cup (1 stick) chilled unsalted butter, cut into small pieces
1 tablespoon cold water
1 teaspoon vanilla

Shelled, toasted and skinned hazelnuts (optional)

Combine nuts, flour, sugar, pepper, salt and aniseed in processor and mix 15 seconds. Add butter and blend using on/off turns until mixture resembles coarse meal. Mix water and vanilla. Add to nut mixture and blend using on/off turns just until dough is moistened; *do not overmix*. Form into ball, wrap in plastic and refrigerate overnight.

Preheat oven to 350°F. Generously butter baking sheet. Roll dough out on floured surface into 9 × 12-inch rectangle about ¼ inch thick. Cut into 1-inch squares. Transfer to prepared baking sheet. Prick top of each square with fork. Top with hazelnut if desired. Bake cookies until golden brown, about 11 to 12 minutes. Let cool on baking sheet about 5 minutes, then cool completely on wire rack. Store in airtight container.

 # *Santa Fe Grill*

Fresh Green Bean Salad
Pepper Seed Thin Breads
Grilled Chicken in Artichoke-Lime Sauce
Barley Pilaf
Almond Butter Cake with Buttercrunch Glaze

Serves 6

Fresh Green Bean Salad

Pine nuts add a nice crunch to this colorful opening course.

6 servings

2 pounds green beans, trimmed

Mustard Vinaigrette
3 tablespoons balsamic vinegar
1 tablespoon coarse-grained mustard
1 teaspoon salt
9 tablespoons olive oil

1 large red onion, peeled, halved and thinly sliced
1 cup toasted pine nuts
Salt and freshly ground pepper

1 large head radicchio
1 large head Bibb lettuce

Cook beans in 2 quarts boiling salted water until crisp-tender, about 7 minutes. Drain. Rinse under cold water and drain well. Pat dry.

For vinaigrette: Combine vinegar, mustard and salt in medium bowl. Slowly whisk in oil in thin stream.

Combine beans, onion and ½ cup pine nuts in large bowl. Mix in vinaigrette. Season with salt and pepper. Let marinate 15 to 30 minutes.

Alternate radicchio and Bibb lettuce leaves over large platter. Mound bean mixture in center. Sprinkle with remaining ½ cup pine nuts and serve.

Pepper Seed Thin Breads

These spicy crackerlike breads are delightful with fruit, cheese or salad. Best served the same day they are made.

Makes 10 breads

½ teaspoon fennel seeds
½ teaspoon aniseed
2¼ cups all purpose flour
1 tablespoon sugar
1 teaspoon salt

1 teaspoon baking powder
½ teaspoon coarsely ground pepper
½ cup water
¼ cup vegetable oil

Bruise fennel and aniseed in mortar with pestle or with rolling pin. Mix with flour, sugar, salt, baking powder and pepper in large bowl. Make well in center of dry ingredients. Add water and oil to well. Gradually draw flour from inner edge of well into center until all flour is incorporated. Knead dough on lightly floured surface until smooth ball forms. Cover with plastic. Let dough rest 15 minutes. (*Can be prepared 1 day ahead and refrigerated.*)

Position rack in center of oven and preheat to 450°F. Grease baking sheet. Divide dough into 10 pieces. Roll 2 pieces into 8-inch rounds (cover remaining dough). Arrange on prepared sheet. Bake until light brown, about 8 minutes. Cool on rack. Continue rolling and baking remaining dough.

Grilled Chicken in Artichoke-Lime Sauce

Soak the cucumber garnish overnight for this unusual main course.

6 servings

2 large cucumbers, peeled, halved and seeded

6 large artichokes, trimmed

2½ cups rich chicken stock
2 shallots, chopped
2½ cups whipping cream

1 tablespoon (about) fresh lime juice
Salt and freshly ground pepper

6 whole chicken breasts, skinned, boned and halved
Vegetable oil
Salt and freshly ground pepper

1 tablespoon oriental sesame oil
1 tablespoon tarragon vinegar

Cut cucumbers into 1½-inch segments. Slice lengthwise as thinly as possible. Soak in ice water overnight.

Set aside 18 artichoke leaves for garnish. Boil artichokes until tender, about 45 minutes. Drain; cool completely. Cut off leaves and save for another use. Scoop out chokes and discard. Set artichoke hearts aside.

Boil chicken stock with shallots in heavy medium saucepan until reduced to 1¼ cups, about 15 minutes. Strain into clean saucepan. Add cream and boil until reduced by ⅓, about 10 minutes.

Puree artichoke hearts in blender. Mix in enough stock-cream mixture to make smooth sauce. Season to taste with lime juice, salt and pepper. Transfer sauce to saucepan. Keep warm.

Prepare barbecue grill with very hot coals. Rub chicken with oil. Season with salt and pepper. Grill chicken on both sides until firm to touch, about 10 minutes, giving chicken ¼ turn when half cooked to create grill marks.

Drain cucumbers thoroughly. Sauté in skillet (preferably nonstick) to warm. Stir in oil, vinegar and pinch of salt.

To serve, spoon sauce onto plates. Top each with 2 chicken breast halves. Garnish with 3 reserved artichoke leaves. Mound cucumbers to side.

Barley Pilaf

8 servings

6 tablespoons (¾ stick) butter
1½ cups chopped leek
   (white part only)
1 cup thinly sliced celery
2 cups pearl barley
   (about 1 pound)
2 bay leaves

1 teaspoon dried thyme, crumbled
1 teaspoon salt
   Freshly ground pepper
3½ cups beef stock
½ cup dry red wine
½ cup minced fresh parsley
¼ cup snipped fresh chives

Preheat oven to 350°F. Melt butter in heavy ovenproof casserole over medium-low heat. Add leek and celery and cook until soft, stirring occasionally, about 6 minutes. Add barley and stir 3 minutes. Add bay leaves, thyme, salt and generous amount of pepper. Mix in stock and wine. Bring to boil. Cover and bake until liquid is absorbed, 35 to 40 minutes. Stir in parsley and chives and serve.

Almond Butter Cake with Buttercrunch Glaze

Makes 1 large tube cake

Glaze
   Butter
⅓ cup unsalted butter
½ cup sliced almonds
¼ cup sugar
¼ cup firmly packed light
   brown sugar
2 tablespoons light corn syrup
½ teaspoon almond extract
2 tablespoons fine dry
   breadcrumbs

Cake
3 cups sifted cake flour
1 teaspoon baking powder

⅛ teaspoon salt
1¼ cups (2½ sticks) unsalted butter,
   room temperature
2 cups sugar
5 eggs, room temperature
1 teaspoon vanilla
⅛ teaspoon almond extract
½ cup milk, room temperature

For glaze: Generously butter 12-cup bundt or tube pan. Melt ⅓ cup butter in heavy small saucepan over medium heat. Add almonds and stir 1 minute. Add sugars, corn syrup and almond extract and stir until sugars dissolve and glaze bubbles, about 2 minutes. Pour into prepared pan, distributing evenly. Dust pan with breadcrumbs.

For cake: Position rack in center of oven and preheat to 350°F. Sift together flour, baking powder and salt. Using electric mixer, beat butter until softened. Gradually add sugar and beat until light and fluffy. Beat in eggs one at a time. Blend in vanilla and almond extract. Beat in dry ingredients and milk alternately, beginning and ending with dry ingredients; do not overmix. Pour batter into prepared pan. Bake until cake is golden brown and tester inserted in center comes out clean, about 1 hour, covering with foil if top browns too quickly. Invert onto rack. Let cool to room temperature.

 # Mesquite Shrimp Barbecue

Fresh Apricot Margaritas
Chèvre Crackers
Watercress Salad with Lemon Dressing
Mesquite-grilled Shrimp with Green Salsa
Green Beans, Asparagus and Snow Peas in Peanut Oil
Lemon-Aniseed Pound Cake

Serves 8

Fresh Apricot Margaritas

Prepare in two batches.

4 servings

Lime slices
Sugar
6 ounces (¾ cup) tequila
1 6-ounce can frozen limeade
2 ounces (¼ cup) apricot brandy
6 ice cubes
3 apricots, peeled, halved and pitted

Rub rims of 4 wine glasses with lime. Dip rims into sugar, coating well. Combine tequila, limeade, brandy, ice cubes and apricots in blender and mix until smooth. Pour into glasses and serve.

Chèvre Crackers

Savory tidbits to enjoy with drinks.

Makes about 3 dozen

½ cup (1 stick) unsalted butter, room temperature
4 ounces mild chèvre (goat cheese), room temperature
2 tablespoons freshly grated Parmesan cheese

1 cup all purpose flour
½ teaspoon salt
Pinch of cayenne pepper

Preheat oven to 375°F. Blend butter and both cheeses in processor until smooth. Add remaining ingredients. Process until just blended using on/off turns. Transfer mixture to pastry bag fitted with medium star tip (No. 4). Pipe in 2-inch-long strips on ungreased baking sheet. Bake until edges begin to brown, about 8 minutes. Cool on rack. Store in airtight container.

Watercress Salad with Lemon Dressing

8 servings

Lemon Dressing
  1 garlic clove
  ¼ cup fresh lemon juice
  2 tablespoons sour cream
  1 tablespoon sugar
  ½ cup safflower oil

  8 ounces watercress, stemmed
  ½ cup grated Monterey Jack cheese (2 ounces)

½ cup fresh blueberries or seedless green grapes
¼ cup chopped toasted pecans

For dressing: Chop garlic in blender. Add lemon juice, sour cream and sugar. With blender running, slowly add oil. (*Dressing can be prepared 1 day ahead and refrigerated.*)

Just before serving, arrange watercress on plates. Drizzle with dressing. Top with cheese, blueberries and pecans.

Mesquite-grilled Shrimp with Green Salsa

The marinade and salsa complement the shrimp perfectly. Tomatillos in the salsa help prevent the avocado from discoloring. Shrimp can be presented in red bell pepper halves.

8 servings

¼ cup safflower oil
¼ cup (½ stick) butter
2 tablespoons chili powder
2 tablespoons fresh lemon juice

1 pound large shrimp, peeled (tail left on) and deveined

6 mesquite chips, soaked in water to cover 30 minutes and drained
Green Salsa*

Prepare barbecue grill with white-hot coals (or set gas grill on high).

Meanwhile, combine oil, butter, chili powder and lemon juice in small saucepan. Stir over medium heat until butter melts. Cool marinade slightly.

Place shrimp in nonaluminum bowl. Add marinade, mixing to coat. Marinate 15 minutes, turning occasionally.

Oil barbecue rack. Add mesquite to coals. Thread shrimp on skewers. Grill until shrimp turn opaque, about 1½ minutes on each side. (*Can be prepared 30 minutes ahead. Wrap in foil and keep at room temperature.*) Serve with salsa.

*Green Salsa

Makes about ³/₄ cup

5 tomatillos,** husked, cored and quartered
1 medium-size green tomato, cored and quartered
2 garlic cloves

1 avocado, peeled, pitted and cut into 1-inch pieces
1 jalapeño pepper, seeded
4 to 5 cilantro sprigs
Salt

Finely chop tomatillos, tomato and garlic in processor using on/off turns. Transfer to heavy medium saucepan. Simmer until beginning to soften, stirring occasionally, about 3 minutes. Pour mixture into blender. Add avocado, jalapeño, cilantro and salt. Blend until smooth, stopping occasionally to scrape down sides of blender, about 3 minutes. (*Can be prepared 1 day ahead and refrigerated.*) Serve at room temperature or slightly chilled.

**Available at Latin American markets.

Green Beans, Asparagus and Snow Peas in Peanut Oil

8 servings

1½ pounds green beans, trimmed
1½ pounds very thin asparagus, trimmed
5½ cups peanut oil (for deep frying)

3 medium garlic cloves, minced
1½ serrano chilies, seeded and minced
6 tablespoons chicken stock

4½ teaspoons soy sauce
1½ teaspoons sugar
6 ounces snow peas, strings removed
Salt and freshly ground white pepper

Pat beans and asparagus dry. Heat oil in wok or heavy deep skillet to 375°F. Add beans and fry until crisp-tender, about 2 minutes. Transfer to paper towels using slotted spoon. Repeat with asparagus; cook about 2 minutes.

Remove all but 1 tablespoon oil from wok. Add garlic and chilies and stir over medium heat 1 minute. Mix in stock, soy sauce and sugar. Add snow peas, beans and asparagus. Toss until vegetables are coated with sauce. Increase heat to high and stir until almost no liquid remains, about 1 minute. Season with salt and pepper and serve.

Lemon-Aniseed Pound Cake

Makes one 4½ × 12-inch loaf

³/₄ cup (1½ sticks) unsalted butter, room temperature
2½ cups sugar
3 eggs, separated, room temperature
5 teaspoons finely grated lemon peel
1½ teaspoons aniseed
1 teaspoon vanilla

2¼ cups all purpose flour
2 teaspoons baking powder
½ teaspoon salt
³/₄ cup milk, room temperature
Pinch of salt
Pinch of cream of tartar
1 tablespoon instant espresso powder

Position rack in center of oven and preheat to 350°F. Grease and flour 4½ × 12-inch loaf pan. Using electric mixer, cream butter and sugar in large bowl until light and fluffy. Beat in yolks one at a time. Blend in peel, aniseed and vanilla.

Sift together flour, baking powder and ½ teaspoon salt. Mix into batter alternately with milk. Using electric mixer with clean dry beaters, beat whites with pinch of salt and cream of tartar in large bowl until stiff but not dry. Fold half of whites into batter to loosen. Fold in remaining whites. Spoon half of batter into prepared pan. Sprinkle evenly with espresso powder. Spoon in remaining batter. Bake until golden brown and tester inserted in center comes out clean, about 1½ hours. Cool 20 minutes in pan. Invert onto rack and cool completely. Chill overnight. Bring to room temperature before slicing.

 Festive Sunset Supper

Sidewinder's Fang
Walnut and Cheese Stuffed Mushrooms
Veal Chops with Pepper-Papaya Relish
Corn grilled in husks
Lancaster Butterhorns
Chocolate Cream Custard

Serves 6

Sidewinder's Fang

6 servings

16 ice cubes
¾ cup fresh lime juice
¾ cup fresh orange juice
¾ cup club soda
¾ cup Puerto Rican golden rum
6 tablespoons Jamaican rum

6 tablespoons 86-proof Demerara rum
¼ cup sugar syrup*
2 tablespoons orgeat syrup*
6 dashes aromatic bitters
6 fresh mint sprigs

Coarsely crush ice cubes in blender. Add all remaining ingredients except mint and mix just until blended. Strain over whole ice cubes in large brandy snifters. Garnish with mint and serve immediately.

*Available in liquor stores.

Walnut and Cheese Stuffed Mushrooms

6 to 8 servings

24 medium mushroom caps
Juice of 1 large lemon

1 teaspoon olive oil
1 teaspoon butter
1 medium onion, minced
3 tablespoons coarsely chopped walnuts
2 green onions, minced
1 small garlic clove, minced
7 ounces fresh spinach, cooked, chopped and squeezed dry

1½ ounces feta cheese, crumbled
1 ounce Gruyère cheese, shredded
2 tablespoons minced fresh dill or 2 teaspoons dried dillweed, crumbled
Salt and freshly ground pepper

1 tablespoon vegetable oil

Toss mushrooms with lemon juice; let stand while making stuffing.

Heat olive oil with butter in heavy medium nonaluminum skillet over medium-low heat. Add onion and cook until soft and transparent. Increase heat to medium-high. Stir in walnuts and cook about 30 seconds. Add green onion and garlic and cook another 30 seconds, stirring constantly. Add spinach and cook briefly until excess moisture has evaporated. Let cool. Stir in cheeses and dill with salt and pepper.

Prepare fire. When coals are very hot, spread sheet of foil over grill and brush with oil. Punch 12 holes into foil.

Meanwhile, stuff mushrooms. Arrange on foil and grill until filling is hot, 8 to 10 minutes. Serve immediately.

Veal Chops with Pepper-Papaya Relish

6 servings

Veal
6 veal chops (about 1 inch thick), trimmed
12 large shallots, blanched and peeled
1 cup safflower oil
¼ cup fresh lime juice
1 tablespoon Worcestershire sauce
2 jalapeño peppers, chopped
3 fresh basil leaves, coarsely chopped
2 garlic cloves, crushed

Relish
1 tablespoon vegetable oil
2 tablespoons minced onion

2 red bell peppers, roasted, peeled, seeded and cut into ¼-inch cubes
1 large poblano chili, roasted, peeled, seeded and cut into ¼-inch cubes
1 tablespoon white wine vinegar
1 lime, halved
Pinch of sugar
Salt and freshly ground pepper
1 large ripe papaya, peeled and cut into ¼-inch cubes

Watercress

For veal: Arrange veal chops and shallots in nonaluminum pan. Combine oil, lime juice, Worcestershire, jalapeños, basil and garlic. Pour over veal and shallots. Marinate 1 hour at room temperature, turning occasionally.

Meanwhile, prepare relish: Heat oil in heavy small skillet over medium heat. Add onion and stir until slightly softened, about 7 minutes. Cool completely.

Add bell peppers, chili and vinegar to onion. Squeeze in juice of ½ lime. Add sugar, salt and pepper. Gently stir in papaya. Adjust seasoning with lime, sugar, salt and pepper.

Prepare barbecue with very hot coals. Remove veal and shallots from marinade, allowing excess to drip off. Grill shallots until tender, about 10 minutes. Grill veal until firm, basting with marinade and seasoning with salt and pepper, about 5 minutes per side.

Set veal chop on each plate. Spoon relish on one side. Set 2 shallots on other. Garnish with watercress and serve.

Lancaster Butterhorns

Makes 3 dozen

1 cup milk
½ cup (1 stick) butter
1 tablespoon sugar
1 teaspoon salt

1 fresh yeast cake

3 eggs, beaten to blend
4½ cups all purpose flour

½ cup (1 stick) butter, melted

Scald milk in heavy large saucepan. Add butter, sugar and salt and stir until butter melts and sugar and salt dissolve. Let cool to lukewarm (95°F).

Crumble yeast cake into milk mixture; let dissolve, then stir to blend. Let stand until foamy, about 10 minutes.

Whisk eggs into milk mixture. Using wooden spoon, stir in flour ½ cup at a time to form soft dough. Turn dough out onto floured surface and knead until smooth and elastic, about 10 minutes. Grease large bowl. Add dough, turning to coat entire surface. Cover with plastic wrap and let rise in warm draft-free area until doubled in volume, 1½ to 2 hours.

Grease baking sheets. Cut dough into 3 pieces. Roll 1 piece out into 9-inch circle. Brush lightly with melted butter. Cut into 12 wedges. Roll each up from base to point to form cylinder. Arrange on prepared sheet. Repeat with remaining dough. (*Can be prepared 1 day ahead and refrigerated.*) Brush dough lightly with melted butter. Cover and let rise until light textured, about 15 minutes. (If dough has been chilled, let rise about 1½ hours.)

Preheat oven to 400°F. Bake butterhorns until golden brown, about 15 minutes. Serve warm or at room temperature.

Chocolate Cream Custard

A perfect do-ahead dessert for either an outdoor or indoor meal.

8 servings

5⅓ cups whipping cream
⅓ cup sugar
8 ounces semisweet chocolate chips, melted

8 egg yolks
Whipped cream and grated chocolate

Preheat oven to 350°F. Combine cream and sugar in top of double boiler set over simmering water and stir until sugar is completely dissolved. Add melted chocolate and blend well. Remove from heat.

Beat yolks in large bowl of electric mixer until fluffy. Gradually beat in chocolate mixture. Divide evenly among eight 8-ounce custard cups. Set cups into shallow pan containing ½ inch hot water. Bake until custard is firm around edges but still creamy in center, about 35 to 40 minutes. Let cool, then chill thoroughly. Garnish with whipped cream and chocolate.

Autumn Knapsack Picnic

Wild Mushroom Bisque
Spiced Apple Bread with Ham and Cheese Stuffing
Carrot, Zucchini and Turnip Salad
Oatmeal Bars with Rum-Raisin Filling

Serves 4 to 6

Wild Mushroom Bisque

6 servings

2 ounces dried morels or porcini mushrooms	Freshly grated nutmeg
3 cups warm water	3 tablespoons all purpose flour
1/4 cup (1/2 stick) unsalted butter	3 cups chicken stock, preferably homemade
1/4 cup chopped shallots	1/2 cup (or more) whipping cream
8 ounces fresh mushrooms, coarsely chopped	Freshly ground white pepper
Salt	1 tablespoon snipped fresh chives

Soak dried mushrooms in warm water until softened, 20 to 30 minutes.

Drain mushrooms, reserving soaking liquid. Rinse mushrooms and squeeze dry. Chop coarsely, discarding any tough stems. Strain soaking liquid through coffee filter and reserve.

Melt butter in heavy large saucepan over medium heat. Add shallots and cook until soft, stirring occasionally, about 3 minutes. Add dried and fresh mushrooms, salt and nutmeg. Cook until most of liquid evaporates, stirring occasionally, 6 to 8 minutes. Add flour and stir 3 minutes. Whisk in stock and 2½ cups mushroom soaking liquid. Bring to boil, whisking constantly. Reduce heat and boil gently until soup thickens slightly, skimming surface occasionally, about 40 minutes.

Whisk ½ cup cream into soup. Simmer 5 minutes; degrease. If desired, thin soup with any remaining mushroom soaking liquid and more cream. Season with salt and pepper. Sprinkle with chives and serve.

Spiced Apple Bread with Ham and Cheese Stuffing

*An aromatic loaf
with a typical Swiss filling.
Superb at breakfast or
brunch as well as for
picnic fare.*

Makes 1 large oval loaf

Apple Bread
1 cup dried apples

2 pounds 2 ounces Golden
    Delicious apples, peeled, cored
    and coarsely chopped
1 cup water
³/₄ teaspoon cracked black pepper
¹/₂ teaspoon freshly grated nutmeg
¹/₂ teaspoon ground coriander
¹/₂ teaspoon cinnamon

1 envelope dry yeast
¹/₄ cup warm water (105°F to 115°F)
1 teaspoon honey

2 tablespoons honey
1 teaspoon salt

2 eggs, beaten to blend, room
    temperature
1 cup whole wheat flour
4 cups (about) unbleached
    all purpose flour

4 ounces paper-thin slices
    Emmenthal cheese
4 ounces paper-thin slices
    prosciutto or cured ham
4 ounces paper-thin slices
    Gruyère cheese

1 egg beaten with 1 tablespoon
    milk (glaze)
2 teaspoons black peppercorns,
    coarsely cracked

For bread: Soak dried apples in warm water to cover 1 hour. Drain and cut apples into ¹/₄-inch cubes.

Combine Golden Delicious apples and 1 cup water in heavy medium saucepan. Cover partially and simmer until apples are very tender, 10 to 15 minutes. Drain well, reserving cooking liquid. Puree apples in processor using on/off turns. Combine 1 cup apple puree (reserve remainder for filling), ³/₄ teaspoon pepper, nutmeg, coriander and cinnamon.

Sprinkle yeast over ¹/₄ cup warm water in small bowl. Add 1 teaspoon honey and stir to dissolve. Let stand until foamy, about 5 minutes.

Add enough water to reserved apple cooking liquid to measure ¹/₂ cup. Combine with seasoned apple puree, yeast, 2 tablespoons honey, salt and dried apples in bowl of heavy-duty electric mixer (can also be made by hand). Blend with dough hook, then mix in eggs. Add whole wheat flour and mix until smooth. Mix in enough all purpose flour 1 cup at a time to form firm, elastic dough that pulls away from sides of bowl. Mix until smooth and shiny, 6 to 7 minutes.

Butter large bowl. Add dough, turning to coat entire surface. Cover with plastic and kitchen towel. Let rise in warm draft-free area until just doubled in volume, about 1¹/₄ hours.

Punch dough down. Knead on lightly floured surface until smooth, 2 to 3 minutes. Cover with kitchen towel and let rest 10 minutes.

Line baking sheet with parchment. Roll and pat dough out on lightly floured surface to 12-inch round. Transfer to prepared sheet, positioning half of dough round in center of sheet (so filled loaf will be centered). Spread half of reserved apple puree over half of dough, leaving 1¹/₂-inch border. Layer Emmenthal, prosciutto and Gruyère over puree, pleating slices to create air spaces (slices should not lie flat) and mounding slightly in center. Spread remaining apple puree over ham and cheese. Brush water on outer 1 inch of dough. Fold dough in half, enclosing filling. Press edges together to seal. Crimp at 1-inch intervals.

Cover bread with kitchen towel. Let rise in warm draft-free area until almost doubled, 30 to 40 minutes.

Position rack in center of oven and preheat to 375°F. Gently recrimp edges of bread. Brush loaf with glaze and sprinkle with 2 teaspoons cracked pepper. Bake until loaf is golden brown and sounds hollow when tapped, about 40 minutes. Cool on rack about 1¹/₂ hours. Serve warm, cutting into long slices or thick wedges.

Carrot, Zucchini and Turnip Salad

Makes 6 cups

12 ounces carrot, cut into julienne
12 ounces turnip, peeled and cut into julienne
12 ounces zucchini, cut into julienne

1 small garlic clove
½ cup fresh parsley leaves

½ cup Vinaigrette*
1 teaspoon dried dillweed

Salt and freshly ground pepper

Place carrot, turnip and zucchini in mixing bowl.
    With machine running, drop garlic through processor feed tube and mince. Add parsley and mince. Add vinaigrette and dill and mix briefly.
    Add vinaigrette mixture to vegetables. Season with salt and pepper.

*Vinaigrette

Makes 2 cups

1½ cups oil (preferably 6 tablespoons French olive oil mixed with safflower oil)
½ cup red wine vinegar

2 teaspoons Dijon mustard
2 teaspoons salt
Freshly ground pepper

Mix all ingredients in processor.

Oatmeal Bars with Rum-Raisin Filling

Replace the rum with orange or pineapple juice for a lunchbox cookie. These are best the day they are baked.

Makes 24

Filling
2 cups raisins (10 ounces)
¾ cup water
¼ cup firmly packed light brown sugar
1 tablespoon fresh lemon juice
5 tablespoons dark rum
½ teaspoon vanilla

Oatmeal Cookie Dough
1½ cups plus 2 tablespoons sifted all purpose flour

½ teaspoon cinnamon
½ teaspoon salt
¼ teaspoon baking soda
1 cup firmly packed light brown sugar
14 tablespoons (1¾ sticks) chilled unsalted butter, cut into ½-inch cubes
¾ teaspoons vanilla
1½ cups quick-cooking oats

½ cup chopped pecans

For filling: Heat raisins, water, sugar and lemon juice in small heavy saucepan over low heat, swirling pan occasionally, until sugar dissolves. Increase heat and bring to boil. Reduce heat and simmer until liquid is reduced to 2 tablespoons, stirring occasionally, about 12 minutes. Cool 10 minutes. Add rum and vanilla, mixing in caramelized sugar on pan bottom. Grind to chunky paste in processor, using about 20 on/off turns. (*Can be prepared 2 days ahead and refrigerated. Bring to room temperature before using.*)
    For dough: Blend flour, cinnamon, salt and baking soda in processor. Mix in sugar. Cut in butter until coarse meal forms, using on/off turns. Add vanilla and process until mixture gathers together, 10 to 15 seconds. Transfer to bowl. Knead in oatmeal. (*Can be prepared 2 days ahead and chilled. Bring to room temperature before continuing.*)
    Position rack in center of oven and preheat to 350°F. Line 9 × 13-inch metal baking pan with foil. Press half of dough evenly into bottom of pan, flattening edges with metal spatula. Bake until brown, about 14 minutes. Place on rack and

press edges again to flatten. Cool 5 minutes. Transfer crust and foil to rack. Let baking pan cool.

Butter same baking pan. Press remaining dough evenly into pan. Press pecans into dough. Bake until slightly darker than first crust, about 16 minutes. Cool in pan on rack until firm but still warm, about 10 minutes.

Spread filling over crust in pan. Gently press first crust onto filling. Cover tightly with foil. Bake 25 minutes. Remove foil and gently press top crust into filling. Cut into 24 bars. Cool at least 1 hour in pan on rack. Recut bars. Serve warm or at room temperature.

 *Oriental Grill*

Plum wine with lime twists
Chicken Broth with Enoki Mushrooms, Green Onions and Ginger
Grilled Salmon Steaks with Watercress-Mustard Butter
Saffron Rice with Snow Peas and Almonds
Kumquat Custard Tartlets

Serves 6

Chicken Broth with Enoki Mushrooms, Green Onions and Ginger

A sophisticated light soup.

6 servings

5 cups chicken stock, preferably homemade
2 tablespoons chopped fresh ginger
⅓ cup thinly sliced green onions
2 ounces enoki mushrooms

2 to 4 tablespoons fresh lime juice
2 tablespoons grated lime peel
　Salt and freshly ground pepper
2 tablespoons minced cilantro

Bring stock and ginger to boil in medium saucepan. Reduce heat, cover and simmer 10 minutes. Strain through fine sieve and return to saucepan. Add green onions, mushrooms, 2 tablespoons lime juice and lime peel. Simmer 5 minutes. Season with salt and pepper. Add more lime juice if desired. Ladle soup into heated bowls. Garnish with cilantro and serve.

Grilled Salmon Steaks with Watercress-Mustard Butter

For an indoor meal the salmon can also be cooked under the broiler.

6 servings

Watercress-Mustard Butter
1 cup watercress leaves, minced
½ cup (1 stick) unsalted butter, room temperature
1 tablespoon minced shallot
1 tablespoon Dijon mustard or to taste

¼ teaspoon salt or to taste
Freshly ground pepper

6 1-inch-thick, 8-ounce salmon steaks
Salt and freshly ground pepper
Watercress sprigs

For butter: Thoroughly combine first 6 ingredients in small bowl. Adjust seasoning. Refrigerate for at least 1 hour. (*Can be prepared 1 day ahead.*)

Adjust barbecue rack 4 inches from fire. Prepare barbecue grill. Season salmon with salt and pepper. Dot with slightly less than half of watercress butter. Arrange buttered side up on rack. Grill 4 minutes. Turn steaks and dot with remaining butter. Cook until just opaque, about 3 minutes. Transfer to plates. Garnish with watercress sprigs and serve immediately.

Saffron Rice with Snow Peas and Almonds

Sesame oil adds an oriental nuance.

6 servings

4 ounces snow peas, trimmed
1 generous pinch saffron threads, crushed
3 cups lukewarm water
2 tablespoons oriental sesame oil
¼ cup chopped onion

1 garlic clove, minced
1½ cups long-grain rice
⅓ cup toasted slivered almonds
3 tablespoons snipped fresh chives
Salt and freshly ground pepper

Blanch snow peas in boiling salted water 30 seconds. Drain and rinse with cold water. Drain well. Cut snow peas diagonally into 2-inch pieces.

Mix saffron and water. Heat oil in heavy medium saucepan over low heat. Add onion and garlic and cook until soft, stirring occasionally, about 6 minutes. Add rice and stir 3 minutes. Mix in saffron water. Increase heat and bring mixture to boil. Reduce heat, cover and simmer until water is absorbed, about 18 minutes.

Stir snow peas, almonds and chives into rice. Season with salt and pepper and serve.

Kumquat Custard Tartlets

6 servings

4 egg yolks, room temperature
⅓ cup sugar
¼ cup Grand Marnier
2 tablespoons grated orange peel
2 cups whipping cream, scalded

6 Tartlet Shells*
6 kumquats in heavy syrup, drained, thinly sliced and seeded
Additional kumquats in heavy syrup, drained (optional)

Beat yolks and sugar to blend in top of double boiler. Stir in Grand Marnier and orange peel. Slowy beat in hot cream. Cook over boiling water until custard thickens and coats back of spoon thickly, stirring frequently. Transfer custard to bowl. Place plastic wrap on surface to prevent skin from forming. Let cool completely. Refrigerate custard until well chilled.

Just before serving, remove tartlet shells from pans. Spoon custard into shells. Arrange kumquat slices atop custard. Garnish plates with additional kumquats if desired.

*Tartlet Shells

Makes six 3-inch tartlet shells

1 cup all purpose flour
6 tablespoons (¾ stick) chilled unsalted butter, cut into small pieces
1 egg yolk

5 teaspoons sugar
1 tablespoon fresh lemon juice
1 tablespoon grated lemon peel
Pinch of salt

Blend all ingredients in processor until mixture begins to gather together; do not form ball. Gather dough into ball; flatten into disc. Wrap in plastic and refrigerate at least 1 hour.

Roll dough out on well-floured surface to thickness of ¼ inch. Arrange six 3-inch diameter tart pans on work surface, sides touching. Place dough over pans, letting it settle into each. Run rolling pin over dough to cut. Fit dough into pans. Pierce dough all over with fork. Refrigerate 2 hours.

Preheat oven to 400°F. Line pastry shells with foil and fill with beans or pie weights. Arrange on baking sheet. Bake 8 minutes. Remove beans and foil. Pierce dough again. Bake until golden brown, about 4 minutes. Cool tartlet shells completely on rack.

Bountiful Greek-style Buffet

Seafood in Ouzo Barbecue
Creamy Eggplant Salad
Leek-filled Porro Bread
Salad Babel with Dill-Mustard Dressing
Rabbit with Onions in Phyllo
Greek Honey Cookies with Walnut-Currant Filling
Toasted Almond Chocolate Cake

Serves 12

Seafood in Ouzo Barbecue

12 servings

20 fresh squid
1½ cups ouzo or anise liqueur
¾ cup fresh lemon juice
2 teaspoons chopped fresh rosemary or 1 teaspoon dried, crumbled
Salt and freshly ground pepper
1½ cups olive oil
36 fresh sea scallops (about 1½ pounds)

24 fresh prawns, shelled and deveined (about 3¼ pounds)
1 onion, cut into wedges and layers separated
3 tomatoes, each cut into 8 wedges
½ lemon

To clean squid: Pull head out of body. Cut head from tentacle cluster and discard with ink sac. Pull out clear skeleton and discard. Rinse cavity. Peel away speckled skin. Cut body into 1-inch rings. Set squid aside.

Mix ouzo, lemon juice, rosemary and salt and pepper in baking dish. Gradually whisk in oil. Add squid, scallops and prawns and marinate about 2 hours, turning occasionally.

Prepare barbecue. Thread seafood (including tentacles), onion and tomatoes evenly onto long skewers. Divide marinade in half. Grill skewers until scallops and shrimp are just cooked through; pierce lemon with fork, dip into half of marinade and use to baste seafood frequently during cooking.

Meanwhile, simmer remaining marinade over medium-high heat until reduced by half. Arrange seafood and vegetables on platter. Pour sauce over. Serve warm or at room temperature.

Creamy Eggplant Salad

Serve with pita bread. The salad can also be prepared in a heavy-duty mixer fitted with paddle attachment.

12 servings

4 large eggplants
(about 6 pounds total)

¼ cup fresh lemon juice
¼ cup minced onion

1 cup olive oil
4 egg yolks, beaten to blend
Salt and freshly ground pepper
Greek olives

Preheat oven to 375°F. Line broiler pan with foil. Arrange eggplants on pan. Prick eggplants 6 to 8 times to allow juices to escape during cooking. Bake until easily pierced, about 1½ hours, turning occasionally.

Preheat broiler. Place eggplants 6 to 7 inches from heat source and broil until charred on all sides. Cool.

Halve eggplants and sprinkle pulp with some lemon juice to prevent discoloration. Scoop some of pulp into large mortar or wooden bowl; discard peel and seeds. Mash in some of remaining lemon juice and onion using pestle. Gradually mash in remaining eggplant, onion and juice, then gradually mash in oil; eggplant should absorb all oil. Blend in yolks, salt and pepper. Turn into serving dish. Top with olives. Chill. Let stand at room temperature for 30 minutes before serving.

Leek-filled Porro Bread

A colossal bread and leek torte, almost like a layered pizza.

12 servings

Dough
¼ cup warm water (80°F to 90°F)
Pinch of sugar
1 tablespoon dry yeast

1¼ cups water
¼ cup vegetable oil
1 tablespoon sugar
1 tablespoon salt
4 cups (or more) unbleached
bread flour

Butter

Leek Filling
3 tablespoons olive oil
2 tablespoons (¼ stick) butter

20 cups chopped leek (white part
and up to 2 inches of green part
of 15 large leeks)

6 ounces smoked ham, cut into
¼-inch cubes
1 cup chopped fresh parsley
Freshly ground pepper
Salt

¾ cup (1½ sticks) butter, melted
12 ounces feta cheese, diced

For dough: Mix water with pinch of sugar in small bowl. Add yeast and let stand until proofed, about 10 minutes.

Mix water, oil, 1 tablespoon sugar and salt in stainless steel electric mixer bowl. Place directly over low heat and stir until lukewarm (about 95°F). Blend in yeast. Mix in 4 cups flour.

Knead dough in mixer fitted with dough hook until smooth, about 6 minutes; dough will be very soft. (*Can also be prepared by hand.*) Continue mixing, adding small amounts of flour, until dough is no longer sticky. Place dough in buttered bowl, turning to coat all sides. Butter top of dough. Cover bowl with kitchen towel and let stand in warm draft-free area until doubled, about 1¼ hours. (Test by making finger indentation of about ¾ inch in center of dough; if dough does not spring back, rising process is completed.)

Butter large baking sheet. Punch dough down. Divide into 3 pieces; pat each into ball, then flatten slightly. Transfer to buttered sheet, spacing evenly. Cover dough with towel and let rise in warm draft-free area until doubled, about 30 minutes.

Meanwhile, prepare filling: Heat oil and butter in heavy 14-inch skillet (or 2 smaller skillets) over medium-high heat. Add leek and sauté until beginning to soften, about 10 minutes, stirring frequently. Reduce heat to medium and cook until all liquid evaporates and leek is cooked through and reduced to 8 to 9 cups, about 15 to 20 minutes.

Add ham, parsley and pepper and cook 5 minutes. Taste and season with salt if necessary. (*Filling can be prepared up to 1 day ahead and refrigerated.*)

Preheat oven to 375°F. Butter 12-inch springform pan. Roll 1 portion of dough out on lightly floured surface into large circle ¼ inch thick. Transfer dough to pan and trim just to fit bottom. Brush about 3 tablespoons melted butter over top. Spread half of leek filling over, then sprinkle with half of cheese. Roll out another portion of dough and arrange in pan; trim excess. Brush with about 3 tablespoons melted butter. Top with remaining filling and cheese. Roll out remaining dough and set over top; trim excess. Brush with remaining butter. Using knife, make several slits through top and middle dough layers; do not pierce bottom. Bake until golden brown, about 1¼ hours. Serve bread warm or at room temperature.

Salad Babel with Dill-Mustard Dressing

12 servings

½ teaspoon salt
2 green onions, finely chopped
3 tablespoons red wine vinegar
1 tablespoon water
1 tablespoon chopped fresh dill
1 tablespoon chopped fresh parsley
1 teaspoon dry mustard
⅛ teaspoon *each* salt and freshly ground pepper
¼ cup corn oil
¼ cup olive oil
1 8½-ounce can (drained weight) artichoke hearts, quartered

1 7¾-ounce can (drained weight) hearts of palm, cut into ¾-inch pieces
1½ heads romaine lettuce (20 ounces), torn into bite-size pieces
3 large tomatoes, cut into wedges
1 large cucumber, halved lengthwise, seeded and cut into ¼-inch slices
¼ cup capers, marinated in wine vinegar 2 days and drained
3 tablespoons dried currants

Sprinkle bottom of salad bowl with ½ teaspoon salt, then rub onions into salt. Blend in vinegar, water, dill, parsley, mustard, remaining salt and pepper. Whisk in oils 1 drop at a time. Before serving, add remaining ingredients and toss thoroughly.

Rabbit with Onions in Phyllo

Gamay Beaujolais makes a suitable beverage— or, if you prefer, try a Greek bottling.

12 servings

8 tablespoons (1 stick) butter
1 tablespoon minced garlic (about 6 medium cloves)
2 small rabbits, cut up (about 4 pounds total)
1 pound firm chorizo sausage (without casing), cut into ¹/₂-inch pieces
4 cups dry white wine
   Salt and freshly ground pepper

2 pounds pearl or boiling onions, peeled
8 ounces small mushrooms
3 celery stalks, cut into ¹/₂-inch cubes (about 1¹/₄ cups)
³/₄ cup rice
³/₄ cup corn oil
³/₄ cup water
1 pound phyllo pastry sheets

Melt 6 tablespoons butter in heavy 14-inch skillet or Dutch oven over medium-high heat. Stir in garlic. Add rabbit and brown lightly on both sides. Add sausage and cook until fat is rendered, about 10 minutes; pour off most of fat. Add 2 cups wine to skillet. Cover and simmer until rabbit is tender, about 10 minutes. Remove rabbit and sausage using slotted spoon; let cool. Remove rabbit meat from bones; cut into ¹/₂ × 1-inch pieces. Season with salt and freshly ground pepper. Set rabbit and sausage aside.

Boil liquid remaining in pan over high heat until thickened and reduced to about 1 cup, about 15 minutes. Add onions, mushrooms and celery and cook until tender, about 10 minutes. Add rice and cook 2 minutes. Blend in remaining 2 cups wine. Add rabbit and sausage and heat through. Remove rice from heat and let stand 20 minutes, stirring occasionally; rice will not be completely tender.

Preheat oven to 350°F. Heat oil with remaining 2 tablespoons butter. Meanwhile, stir water into rabbit. Coat 9 × 14-inch baking dish with some of oil mixture. Line dish with 8 phyllo pastry sheets, brushing each with oil mixture and making sure pastry comes up sides of dish. Pour in rabbit mixture and spread evenly. Fold sides over filling. Top with 6 more oiled phyllo pastry sheets. Tuck pastry under evenly; do not pull too tightly. To facilitate serving, cut top 3 sheets into serving-size squares; do not cut through all layers or liquid will exude during cooking. Bake until golden brown, about 40 minutes. Cool 15 minutes before serving.

Greek Honey Cookies with Walnut-Currant Filling

These very rich treats make the perfect finale to any Greek or Middle Eastern meal. For maximum flavor, start them at least one day ahead.

Makes 36

Filling
³/₄ cup diced toasted walnuts
2 tablespoons (¹/₄ stick) butter
2 teaspoons honey
1¹/₄ teaspoons fresh lemon juice
1 teaspoon finely grated lemon peel
¹/₄ teaspoon cinnamon
²/₃ cup dried currants

Syrup
2 cups sugar
1 cup water
²/₃ cup honey
1 tablespoon fresh lemon juice
10 whole cloves
1 3-inch cinnamon stick
1 ³/₄-inch piece vanilla bean

Dough
3 cups sifted all purpose flour
¹/₂ cup regular Cream of Wheat cereal
2 teaspoons baking powder
1 teaspoon cinnamon
³/₄ teaspoon salt
¹/₂ teaspoon ground cloves
10 tablespoons (1¹/₄ sticks) unsalted butter, room temperature
¹/₂ cup vegetable oil
¹/₂ cup sugar
2¹/₂ tablespoons fresh lemon juice
2¹/₂ tablespoons Cognac
1 teaspoon vanilla
¹/₂ cup coarsely ground walnuts

For filling: Blend 2 tablespoons walnuts, butter, honey, lemon juice, peel and cinnamon in processor until smooth. Transfer to bowl. Stir in remaining walnuts and currants. Cover and refrigerate until ready to use. (*Can be prepared 2 days ahead.*)

For syrup: Heat all ingredients in heavy small skillet over low heat until sugar dissolves, swirling pan occasionally. Increase heat and bring to boil. Reduce heat and simmer until slightly thickened, about 10 minutes. Cool completely. Refrigerate until ready to use. (*Can be prepared 2 days ahead.*)

For dough: Mix flour, Cream of Wheat, baking powder, cinnamon, salt and cloves in bowl. Using electric mixer, cream butter while drizzling in oil in thin stream. Gradually beat in sugar. Blend in lemon juice, Cognac and vanilla. Stir in dry ingredients. Let dough stand 10 minutes before using.

To assemble: Position rack in center of oven and preheat to 350°F. Line baking sheets with foil. Shape dough into 36 smooth ¼-inch-wide rounds. Press finger down center of each round to form gully; cookie should be 2½ to 3 inches long and 2 to 2½ inches wide. Spoon rounded teaspoon of filling into each gully. Carefully fold dough over filling to enclose completely. Shape cookie to resemble date. Arrange cookies on prepared sheets. Bake until golden brown, about 25 minutes. Transfer to rack and cool completely. (*Can be prepared 2 days ahead. Cover cookies loosely and store at room temperature.*)

Bring syrup to simmer. Immerse cookies in batches in syrup 1 minute, turning once. Transfer to rack using slotted utensil. Sprinkle each cookie with 1 teaspoon ground walnuts. Refrigerate until very cold. Arrange on tray. Cover loosely. Let stand at room temperature 1 to 2 days to mellow.

Toasted Almond Chocolate Cake

The texture of this rich dessert is between a pudding and a cake.

12 servings

1⅔ cups blanched slivered almonds, well toasted and ground (1½ cups ground)
6 ounces semisweet chocolate, coarsely chopped
½ cup (1 stick) unsalted butter, cut into ½-inch cubes
¼ cup milk

5 eggs, separated, room temperature
1 cup plus 6 tablespoons powdered sugar
6 tablespoons brandy
1 tablespoon very finely ground espresso coffee beans or instant coffee powder

1 tablespoon all purpose flour
1 teaspoon almond extract

¾ cup brandy
½ cup plus 2 tablespoons orange marmalade (with peel)
6 ounces semisweet chocolate
¼ cup milk
1 teaspoon espresso beans, very finely ground
3 tablespoons vegetable oil

Combine almonds, chocolate, butter and milk in medium skillet over very low heat and stir until chocolate is melted and smooth. Cool.

Meanwhile, set rack in upper position of oven and preheat to 350°F. Butter 10-inch springform pan. Beat yolks with half of powdered sugar in large bowl of electric mixer until pale and slowly dissolving ribbon forms when beaters are lifted. Beat whites in another large bowl until stiff but not dry, adding remaining half of sugar gradually. Slowly stir yolks into cooled chocolate mixture. Blend in 6 tablespoons brandy, coffee, flour and almond extract. Gently fold in large spoonful of whites to lighten, then gently fold in remaining whites. Pour batter into prepared pan. Bake about 35 minutes (5-inch area in center of cake will be very moist). Cool cake completely on wire rack.

To serve, invert cake onto plate with slightly raised edge. Warm remaining brandy in small saucepan; ignite and shake pan gently until flames subside. Pour brandy evenly and slowly over cake. Spoon marmalade in thin layer over top of cake, leaving ½-inch border. Melt remaining chocolate with milk and espresso in small saucepan over low heat. Stir in oil. Spoon chocolate onto border and let run down sides, covering completely and forming pool on plate.

Can be prepared 1 day ahead; store at room temperature.

🍎 *Index*

Credits and Acknowledgments

The following people contributed the recipes included in this book:

Ann's Plum, Hagerstown, Maryland
Margot Bachman
Michele Braden
Jennifer Brennan
Janet Brown
Mary Bryant
Giuliano Bugialli
Karen Butterfield
Cabell's, Charleston, South Carolina
George Caloyannidis
Molly Chappellet
Barbara Clausen
Ruth Comstock
Patricia Connell
Donna Dinova
Meryl Dun
Sue Ellison
Joe Famularo
Dean Fearing
Sherry Ferguson
Peggy Glass
David Grant
Bob and Beverly Green
Mary Green
Freddi Greenberg
Tori Griffin
Hugh Grogan
Cathy and Don Hagen
Lyn Heller

Beth Hensperger
Holbrooke Company, Grass Valley,
    California
Jerry House
Sally Jordan
Jane Helsel Joseph
Barbara Karoff
Lynne Kasper
Kristine Kidd
Mai-Kai, Fort Lauderdale, Florida
Saleh Makar
Abby Mandel
Joel McCormick
Michael McLaughlin
Jefferson Morgan
Jinx Morgan
Selma Morrow
Joanne O'Donnell
Lori Openden
Pat Opler
Papagayo, San Diego, California
Pat and Steve Pepe
George Perry-Smith
Martha Peters
Carolyn Reagan
Mary Nell Reck
The Restaurant in Fort Bragg,
    Mendocino, California
Lucy Rice

Elizabeth Riely
Phyllis Rizzi
Michael Roberts
Neil Romanoff
Betty Rosbottom
Susan Sandler
Richard Sax
Gillian Servais
Edena Sheldon
Wendy Silverman
Jerry Slaby
Shirley Slater
Lyn Stevens
Rita Sugarman
Christine Tittel
Daryl Trainor
Mark Trevor
Nicole Urdang
Gregory Usher
Suneeta Vaswani
Charlotte Walker
Sheri Wayne
Janie Wilson
Jan Wilton
Jo-Ann Zbytniewski

Additional text was supplied by:
Lynne Kasper, *Hints for the
    Charcoal Chef*

The Knapp Press
is a wholly owned subsidiary of
KNAPP COMMUNICATIONS CORPORATION.

Composition by Publisher's Typography

This book is set in Sabon, a face designed by Jan Teischold in 1967 and based on early fonts
engraved by Garamond and Granjon.